MW01406330

Copyright

TruthSeekah
Spirit Realm

Angels, Demons, Spirits and the Sovereignty of God

Foreword by Jordan Maxwell

COPYRIGHT

Spirit Realm | Angels, Demons Spirits and the Sovereignty of God by TruthSeekah

Published by TruthSeekah
P.O. Box 333 Creola Al, 36525
www.TruthSeekah.com

Copyright © 2019 TruthSeekah

Scripture taken from the New King James Version®. Copyright © 1982 by Thomas Nelson. Used by permission. All rights reserved.

All rights reserved. No portion of this book may be reproduced in any form without permission from the publisher, except as permitted by U.S. copyright law. For permissions contact:
TruthSeekah7@yahoo.com

Cover by Costea Mihai

ISBN: 978-0-578-59405-7

Spirit Realm: Angels, Demons, Spirits and the Sovereignty of God

Copyright

Spirit Realm: Angels, Demons, Spirits and the Sovereignty of God

TABLE OF CONTENTS

CONTENTS

Copyright 4
Table of Contents 8
Foreword by Jordan Maxwell 16
Introduction 23
Part 1 The Sovereignty of God 27
   Trials, Tribulations and Testing 32
   Simon the Sorcerer and the Anointing 34
Part 2 Angels, Spirits and Demons 37
   A Spirit Passed Before My Face 37
   The Witching Hour 41
   Evil Spirits Sent From God 42
   The Angel of The Lord 44
   Spirits Don't Die 44
   Fallen Angels 49
   Spirituality and Hair 51
   Sleep Paralysis and Shadow People 53
Part 3 Familiar Spirits and Channeling 57
   Ventriloquist / Channeling 57
   Reincarnation 63
   Communing With The Dead 65
   Scapegoat 67
Part 4 Beings of Light 73
   Satan: An Angel of Light? 76
   Angelic Contact 78

Novena 86
Part 5 Aliens, Angels and UFOs 89
Chariots of Fire 90
The CE5 Contact Initiative Summoning Angels / UFOs .92
By The Stars of Orion 95
Over My House 97
The Divine In Art..99
Part 6 Plant Medicine 103
Manifestation 108
The Golden Teachers 112
Part 7 Entering The Trance State 117
The Bible and The Trance State 117
Opening The Third Eye...121
Chanting 122
Meditation 123
Music...123
Burning Incense 124
Synchronicity..124
Part 8 Elemental Spirits 127
Fairy Encounter 130
Elemental Spirits and Golems 131
Attacked by an Elemental Shade 133
Part 9 Symbols, Signs & Sigils 139
The Teraphim 143
Cursed Objects 144
Blessed Objects 144
Crystals 146
Ephod..147

Table of Contents

- Magical Staffs 148
- Part 10 Divination 151
  - Jonah 154
  - Joseph and Matthias 154
  - Urim and Thummin 157
  - Intention 157
- Part 11 Who Is Lucifer? 159
- Part 12 Fasting To Rid One's Self of Spirits 163
  - Parasites and Dragons 166
  - Teratoma Tumors 170
- Part 13 Overcoming Evil Spirits (James 4:7) 173
- Part 14 Jesus 179
  - The Light of Christ 182
- Part 15 Spiritual Giftings and Psychic Abilities 185
  - The Woman at the Well 189
  - Clairvoyance (Clear Seeing) 192
  - Clairscent (Clear Smelling) 194
  - Clairaudience (Clear Hearing) 195
  - Claircognizance (Clear Knowing) 197
  - Clairsentience (Clear Feeling) 200
- Part 16 List of Spirits Mentioned and Their Functions 205
  - Spirit of Adoption 205
  - Spirit of fear; Power, Love, Sound Mind 206
  - Fear 206
  - Power 206
  - Love 207
  - A Sound Mind 208
  - Deaf, Dumb & Foul Spirit 209

- Foul Spirit ... 210
- Spirit of Heaviness ... 211
- Spirit of Whoredom ... 212
- Haughty Spirit ... 212
- Spirit of Antichrist ... 213
- Spirit of Divination or Python ... 213
- Unclean Spirit ... 214
- Spirit of Slumber ... 214
- Spirit of Error ... 215
- Spirit of Jezebel ... 216
- Familiar Spirit ... 216
- Spirit of Infirmity ... 217

References and Citations ... 220
Notes and Journaling ... 222
About The Author ... 234

Spirit Realm: Angels, Demons, Spirits and the Sovereignty of God

Witches, wizards, sorcery, evil and unclean spirits, devils, ghosts, demonic possession and exorcisms, conjuring up and raising the dead, divination, trances, astrology, oracles, enchantments, supernatural healing, super-human strength, giants, dragons, and unicorns are but a few of the many instances of paranormal phenomena found in the Bible. Some of the lesser known anomalies in scripture are: levitation, astral projection, clairvoyance, psychokinesis, telepathy, metamorphosis, glossalia, behemoths, satyrs, cockatrices, flying fiery serpents, and gigantic and terrifying, fire-breathing, smoke-snorting, stone-hearted, indestructible, amphibious sea monsters. This research work is intended to provide evidence that not all of these paranormal anomalies are properly understood or, are completely misrepresented, by the church and mainstream thought. There has long been a gulf between the church's portrayal of these seemingly unnatural things and the beliefs of many others outside the sphere of dogmatic interpretation.

Patrick Cooke | 1949 - 2012

Spirit Realm: Angels, Demons, Spirits and the Sovereignty of God

FOREWORD BY JORDAN MAXWELL

I've been asked to do a forward in TruthSeekah's new book, Spirit Realm | Angels Demons and the Sovereignty of God and the reason why I was asked to do the forward is because I have spent over 60 years of my life in the world that he is writing about. I am well aware of the world of the spiritual and the occult and hidden world of the spirits that TruthSeekah is writing about in this book, and believe me, there is this spirit world and all of mankind has always understood that. Native Americans talked about the great spirits, all the ancient people in the Middle East talked about the spirits, the Orientals talk about the spirits, the Occidentals, the Chinese. All the ancient cultures of the world have talked about the spirit beings, the devils, the demons, the angels, the poltergeist etc. The motion pictures today and television shows are replete with spiritual implications of unseen spirits, the invisible man, so to speak.

I'm happy to be able to add my two cents to the great book that needs to be written. There is a spiritual pecking order going up into the heavens. And there was a book put out many years ago by Hesiod entitled "The Theogony of Hesiod" which was a very ancient book going back into the ancient Grecian Empire in which Hesiod was told to write the book about the pecking order of the gods in the heavens. And this is a very important and ancient subject that needs to be reviewed today happily I'm part of the book that's doing just that. You need to pay attention closely while reading the contents of this work think about what you're going to read in this book.

Spirit Realm: Angels, Demons, Spirits and the Sovereignty of God

The earth is a stage and upon that stage are many characters, actors and scenarios that all serve the greater play. There are people who are considered to be your enemies in this world who may not really be your enemies at all and it may just be their role in the play. This is also true for the many wars around the world, which are all set up, organized and financed by the same people. When we go into war in America, we have different theaters of war. You had the Pacific theater; you had the European theater of war etc. The word "Theater" implies that it's a show. This is also the same scenario as when you see the two boxers or the two fighters that go into the ring in Las Vegas and hundreds of thousands are watching the fight from all over the world yet nobody seems to realize the mafia is the one making all the money. Somebody put up the millions of dollars to get the hotel and to finance the organization of the fight and put it on television and control the gambling and the betting. The two fighters who are fighting are trying to kill each other and beat each other up are actually just employees of a corporation. They are being paid well for what they are doing. It's all part of the job. That's why the mob has always used that term, "nothing personal, it's just business".

That's what the world of mankind is, it's a business and therefore the guys who you think are your enemies are not , it's just a business. They're being paid to look like your enemy. The same people who are paying you to go out and fight are the same people who are paying them to go out and fight. So, you're going into the ring with an opponent. Our opponent was Adolph Hitler in the Second World War. He was just one more pawn in the game being played on the world. You need to realize the world is a game and it goes all the way back to thousands of years. There is a pecking order in the spirit world and this is what most people have lost because of what we call our Marxian and Marxist thinking. Marxian thinking as says, there is no spirit world, we're all just humble members of a corporation and we all have to crawl on our knees to the organization headquarters. Well, there's another part of the world that says, no, we are humans. We come from somewhere out there and that there is a spirit world operating out there in the universe and all around us in this massive, massive spiritual matrix that's at work.

We are at war right now with the concept of Marxian ideology. Carl Marx gave us the idea that there's nothing holy, nothing, that we're just owned and operated by corporations to which I say no, that is nothing more than communist philosophy. There is in point of fact, a spiritual world out there and we as subservient to it. I know that to be true because I've been there and seen it with my own eyes.

TruthSeekah also covers the subject of angels, demons and disembodied spirits. There are different kinds of spirit creatures in the aethers. Some are actually angels and some have been in human bodies and have left hence being referred to as disembodied spirits. They used to be in a body but when the human died, the spirit left the body causing a disembodied spirit that wants to get back into a body because that's where it is more comfortable. This is also where the idea about reincarnation comes from. Some believe that when you die, your spirit is very uncomfortable being in the spirit world and it wants to get back into the spin of things on the earth. The spirit waits for that right time for the right person to be born and then it jumps into that person's body. The idea of reincarnation is that there are disembodied spirits that want to come back into human bodies. I actually think there is something to that. It shows us that there are other spirits out there in the world that affect us other than only angels and demons. These beings are like angels in that they're spirit creatures, but they used to be in a body. Now that they're no longer in a body they don't know what to do with themselves. So, they need to come back in and be a part of the human family again, so they reincarnate.

Elemental spirits are different, elemental spirits are really strange. I've actually seen elementals. I've had one on one experiences with them. I don't know exactly what they are, all I know is what to call them, but I've had incidents where I have been in the company of elementals. They are spirit creatures, like fairies and leprechauns. I have seen Leprechauns, Gnomes and fairies and these are what we call the elementals. They are legitimate life forms but they don't live in this world like you do. They live in a different kind of world, an elemental world, so we call them the elementals. What is life like in the spirit world? That's what you're going to read about in this book.

The Apostle Paul says in the scriptures that there is a war inside of each one of us. This war is between God and the devil both dwelling inside of us. This is talking about our Elohim nature versus our Neanderthal nature. The Neanderthal, or fallen, nature is drinking in bars, raping, fighting and doing other sin-nature things, the way the animals lived. The Elohim nature, or godly, nature is the other part of us that can understand beautiful music, poetry, design lasers, create motion pictures, build rockets and do all of the other wonderful things that our brains are capable of. That is the god part, or the extraterrestrial part of us. Each one of us is half animal, half spirit.

You must choose daily between the two natures and force yourself to be to live in your ascended nature not to be like the animals. Anyone can go out, get drugged up, kill somebody and rape and plunder until one day they become like Charlie Manson in that they're so animalistic and crazy from feeding the lower nature.

There is something to the idea that there are demonic spirit entities that watch us and they see how we live, how we feed ourselves, our sex drive etc. They see how we live and they want to live like us. These entities see that we roam around free and do whatever we want to do and they'd like to come and be like us. I think that they probably do try and intervene in our evolution and become part of the human family. In doing so they are coming into a situation that they were not designed to be in.

People fantasize about joining the secret societies that deal with the extraterrestrials, spirits and demons. We are to stay out of those types of societies that deal with the demonic realms of human sacrifices, the blood rituals and all that demonic stuff. We're supposed to be different than that. We're supposed to be more intelligent and better than that. But I do think that there is some kind of a connection between us and the demonic realm.

The whole human family is dying because of a lack of knowledge. We are like a disease on this earth. We are raping and killing each other, destroying the planet that we're on and we don't seem to be able to stop or slow down the destruction that we're part of. This is the reason that I think it is important that this kind of book be out there to express and to explain how we humans are being misled by spiritual entities. It's a very important subject and it needs to be reintroduced into Western civilization. There is a spiritual world and we are subjected to it. I know because I've seen it. I've been a part of it. People have experiences every day in their life with spirits, but they don't do anything about it. They just have experiences and they know they've had an experience. Winston Churchill once said, "Normally a person in his life will come across a spiritual experience which will knock him off his feet, but most people will just get up and brush themselves off and go about their business and never even think about it". If you have some kind of a spiritual experience that just frightened you or knocked you off your feet you better think about that. What was it? Why did it happen to you? And when you talk about some kind of a spiritual experience, that's not of this world, don't just get up and brush yourself off and go off and go and do what you were going to do before. You better think about that spiritual experience.

That's what this book is doing; it's causing people to understand for the first time that we are part a spiritual ecosystem of life forms out there in the universe.

Foreword by Jordan Maxwell

Introduction

I have made it my life's purpose to understand the spirit world and how it operates. I have long been intrigued by how we are affected by unseen forces that are at work in and around us at all times. As a teenager this led me down the path of occult studies, not only reading esoteric and satanic books but performing the rituals that accompanied them. It was my desire to reach into the void and make contact, simply to know that something else existed. This fascination stemmed from having encounters with shadow beings in my bedroom as a child. Reaching out by mixing Wiccan, Satanism and Necromancy rituals I can honestly say that I just wasn't ready for what was going to reach back. Doing this opened up a portal to a spirit realm full of entities that brought torment deep into my being. This led me down a path of disillusion and schizophrenia. I was pulled in and out of trances by the will of all the spirits I had given permission to inhabit my body. I began to get very ill, coughing up blood, having voices in my head, speaking foreign languages and seeing spirits running through my home in the night. I knew that if I was to try and get help from a doctor they would think that I was insane and give me meds or have me committed. I became a Christian a few years before and remembered the peace that I had in the presence of God, yet at this point I felt so far away. In a last effort of desperation, I asked my girlfriend to pray with me that God would heal me and deliver me from the torments of these wicked spirits. The next day I felt a lot better so I opened up the phonebook to find churches to call looking for help. I called and left voicemails on their answering machines saying that I needed prayer because I thought I was demon possessed. I called around maybe fifteen churches in total and only one called me back. We ended up meeting with a pastor who came to our house to pray with us and I

Introduction

devoted my life back to following God on September 7, 2000. Since then my journey has been amazing, full of ups and downs and everything in between. I began to study the spiritual giftings in the Bible and I saw that the Bible is of full stories where Jesus and the disciples used what we would call supernatural powers or psychic abilities. As I fasted and prayed, I had ecstatic encounters with God and felt the Holy Spirit rush through my home and even do a deep inner work within me to bring healing to my soul. These encounters began to increase over the years and I began to go deeper in my studies of the Bible and my personal pursuit to find a similar practice to that of Jesus and the disciples. I longed for a Biblical Christianity before it was tampered with by Constantine and the Catholic Church. The Christianity of today looks nothing like the Christianity of the Bible. Christianity started out as a spiritual practice or connection with God in the East and then became a Religion in the West. My pursuit has led me to study many braches and offshoots of Christianity looking for the one that was the closest to the original doctrines. Again my intrigue led me to study and fellowship with many different people groups and sects that seemed to have a bit more truth than the former. This study led me in and out of many doctrines, theologies and schools of thought all claiming to hold the truth and demonizing those who thought differently. I studied under the Pentecostal Assemblies of God Church, then got involved with Messianic Judaism and learned to try and keep the law. We actually started eating a Kosher diet and withdrew from all of the Babylonian Holidays (Christmas, Easter, Halloween and etc.) and started to keep the Biblical Feasts and Sabbaths. This then led me down the path of the Hebrew Israelites and then back into Non-denominational Church where I continued to study Biblical theology and doctrine. What I ended up coming to realize was that none of the churches or denominations had THE TRUTH but they all held a beautiful part of the truth that they each practiced very well. They all had something that set them apart. Each had something that made them look a little closer to the real thing than the next, but they (like every person or religion) also had these weird character flaws or holes in their doctrines that negated what little truth that they had. Throughout this ten year pursuit I acquired a lot of knowledge and experience. I made it my personal goal to hang on to the good and release the bad. During this transition of my studies, I continued to have amazing supernatural revelations and downloads in the presence of God. I came to a place of supernatural resting from dead works when I eventually gave up my "right to be right". In this I found much peace because I had become so combative when it came to the Bible or Truth throughout those studies. I began to go deeper in my spiritual awakening and started to see God through a bigger lens. I started researching books that were taken out of the Bible and even referencing other religious texts and I began to see links and similarities that tie us all together. I saw that the majority of us were saying the same thing only wording it differently. This was huge a breakthrough for me because in Christianity I was taught to study these religions and find out what makes us different but here I was overwhelmed by what made us all the same. There is an honest pursuit in the heart of man for knowledge, adventure and to know their creator. Most of these other religions are just working with what they were given and doing the best they can. This worldview led me deeper into the Bible and actually gave me a better understanding of many of the cryptic meanings of obscure scriptures and dark sayings held within it. All the while I was still continuing to have spiritual encounters and experiences in the realm of the divine, seeing miracles, healings and ecstatic encounters with the Holy Spirit. At this point I ended up back where I started. I still wanted to know how the spirit world works and operates and I studied this from both sides, the light and the dark, and they both exist simultaneously. The universe works in such a way with our consciousness that you find what you are

Introduction

looking for. If you look for the bad in a person or situation you will surely find it. If the good is what you're seeking, then that is what you'll find. As a man thinketh in his heart so shall he be.

This body of work is intended to help you grow in your knowledge of how the spirit realm works and operates. Hosea 4:6 says "My people are destroyed for a lack of knowledge". We find this to be true in many areas of life. This book focuses on the reality of the closeness of the spirit realm. If we can understand how the etheric realm not only operates, but communicates and even influences humans, then this will help us better interact with the spirits that be. This interaction is something that is happening by default and many people fall victim due to their own lack of knowledge and misunderstandings. With better insight into the spirit realm, we find ourselves fighting a spiritual battle that is at hand. The majority only seem to play defense. They only react to attack. They are never on the offense and never take the right precautions to achieve victory in their own life, much less the lives of their friends, family or people around them. Having proper knowledge increases our faith and vision and allows us to see an outcome before it is even conceived.

PART 1
THE SOVEREIGNTY OF GOD

Viktor Vasnetsov God of hosts (1885-1896)

There is a natural order to all things. Everything in creation works together in unity and is a part of facilitating our existence. The same is true with the order of God and the spirit realm. The sovereignty of God shows us that everything works together for a purpose; the good, the bad and everything in between. In my research I have seen people who do not understand the sovereignty of God come up with many different ideas trying to understand the duality of God. Many have fallen to Gnosticism which believes that the God of the Old Testament is a totally different entity than the New Testament God. I believe that this stems from a lack of understanding of God's complexity and dualistic nature. It is only in darkness that we are able to appreciate the light. We must understand that life isn't black and white. Life is

Part 1
The Sovereignty of God

an entire spectrum with gradients and color frequencies. In Isaiah 45:7 God says "I form the light, and create darkness: I make peace, and create evil: I the LORD do all these things." This can be a hard pill to swallow when we have been told all of our lives that it was the devil that created evil in the world. The angelic order works like this; when God says something or orders it to be done, angels, demons and spirits go fourth to carry out the will of God. There are angels over specific seasons and months as well as spirits over the elemental kingdoms as well. In times of trouble, calamity or refreshing, spirits are loosed from heaven into the earth to bring about their essence. It is God who binds and looses them from their heavenly habitation to interact with mankind.

Below is an example out of 1st Kings 22:21 where the sons of God appeared before the Lord with ideas of how to chastise the prophets. As they descend, the essence of the spirits changes the vibration of people groups, kings and nations on an individual or collective basis.

AND THERE CAME FORTH A SPIRIT, AND STOOD BEFORE THE LORD, AND SAID, I WILL PERSUADE HIM. AND THE LORD SAID UNTO HIM, WHEREWITH? AND HE SAID, I WILL GO FORTH, AND I WILL BE A LYING SPIRIT IN THE MOUTH OF ALL HIS PROPHETS. AND HE SAID, THOU SHALT PERSUADE HIM, AND PREVAIL ALSO: GO FORTH, AND DO SO. NOW THEREFORE, BEHOLD, THE LORD HATH PUT A LYING SPIRIT IN THE MOUTH OF ALL THESE THY PROPHETS, AND THE LORD HATH SPOKEN EVIL CONCERNING THEE. | 1KINGS 22:21

STAY YOURSELVES, AND WONDER; CRY YE OUT, AND CRY: THEY ARE DRUNKEN, BUT NOT WITH WINE; THEY STAGGER, BUT NOT WITH STRONG DRINK. FOR THE LORD HATH POURED OUT UPON YOU THE SPIRIT OF DEEP SLEEP, AND HATH CLOSED YOUR EYES: THE PROPHETS AND YOUR RULERS, THE SEERS HATH HE COVERED. | ISAIAH 29:9-10

In understanding the spirit realm, angels, demons, spirits and their functions, we must understand the sovereignty of God and how he uses all things to bring glory to His name. There is nothing that happens that God does not see and there is nothing that happens that is outside of the will of God. God uses every situation for His glory and ultimately for our good. This can be through trials and tribulations which are oftentimes aided by spirits sent from God himself. We are shown in several instances in the Old Testament where the spirits present themselves before God to take orders and to carry out deeds upon the earth. In Job 1:6 we see the angels presenting themselves himself before God with Satan being in the midst of them.

NOW THERE WAS A DAY WHEN THE SONS OF GOD CAME TO PRESENT THEMSELVES BEFORE THE LORD, AND SATAN CAME ALSO AMONG THEM.
AND THE LORD SAID UNTO SATAN, WHENCE COMEST THOU? THEN SATAN ANSWERED THE LORD, AND SAID, FROM GOING TO AND FRO IN THE EARTH, AND FROM WALKING UP AND DOWN IN IT. AND THE LORD SAID UNTO SATAN, HAST THOU CONSIDERED MY SERVANT JOB, THAT THERE IS NONE LIKE HIM IN THE EARTH, A PERFECT AND AN UPRIGHT MAN, ONE THAT FEARETH GOD, AND ESCHEWETH EVIL? | JOB 1:6

Satan along with any other spirits must seek permission from God before they act upon the earth. The meaning of the word Satan means "Adversary" or "Opponent of that that which is good". Just like we are able to play many roles of the Biblical archetypes in our lives, we can also play the role of a satan as well. In Mark 8:33 we see Peter oppose the will of Jesus and try to make alterations to his destiny and Jesus suddenly rebukes him saying "Get thee behind me, Satan: for thou savourest not the things that be of God, but the things that be of men".

Part 1
The Sovereignty of God

The Satan figure is not Gods enemy, he is ours. Satan does not think that one day he will overthrow God the Father and take his throne. He knows his place. He is a created being or force that is used to bring chastisement to humans. In some circles the Satan is venerated because he is used to get one ready for Christhood, bringing about the tribulation and trouble needed to show one's self approved. The angelic orders all work in harmony with one another. Things may seem a bit more complicated with this belief. If these spirits are sent to us from God, then which spirits do we cast out and rebuke and which spirits are sent here to teach us? The answer is that all spirits are here to teach. If one opens themselves up to demonic influence leading to possession or oppression, once the individual is rid of the spirit, they must "learn" how to keep that door shut. The individual must walk in holiness and integrity in that area or they will continue to open themselves up for the spirit to return to them with seven spirits greater and even more wicked. This is hands on learning and is the root of all Gnosis
(Knowledge gained through experience).

Let us look at a few more scriptures that explain this in further detail. In 2 Corinthians 12:7 the apostle Paul speaks about a man who was having other worldly revelations and encounters in the spirit realm, so much so that the man began to be looked upon as special or holy. This began to produce pride in his heart. He says it was given to him "a thorn in the flesh". This was an infirmity sent to him by a messenger of Satan to buffet him, lest he should be exalted above measure. It is debatable as to what this "thorn in the flesh" was, but many scholars believe that Paul's vision was failing him, yet this is not known for sure. What we can know from this passage of scripture is that the term used says that it was a "messenger of Satan" that was sent to him. A "messenger of Satan" is what we would call a demon or demonic entity. The word angel simply translates to messenger, and infirmity translates to sickness. The angels or spirits carry messages and this message was to remain humble and not become lifted up with pride. The scripture says that "pride cometh before a fall" in Proverbs 16:8. Paul then begins to seek the Lord about this spirit of infirmity and on three occasions he asked God to take it away from him, yet the Lord replied "My grace is sufficient for thee: for my strength is made perfect in weakness." Paul then understood the message and knew that even though he may be suffering in body, it was in his weakness that Christ was glorified. We can all praise God when things are going great, but can we praise Him in the midst of the storm when it seems like all is lost? This was the message for Paul and for us as well.

There is nothing happening without God knowing it and even orchestrating it. This can be hard to understand as we see things that are negative or uncomfortable for us as demonic or evil. We may say to ourselves, "How can a loving God allow evil to happen?" This is the sovereignty of God. The scriptures tell us that it is through resistance and tribulations that character is formed. It is the testing of our faith that shows what we really believe. All things work together for the good of those who love God. There is beauty in the blueprint as we learn to trust God and the process thereof. The Lord is not divided, duality is not schizophrenia but indeed all things fit together cohesively. There is no light without darkness, there is no positive without negative, there is no day without night and there is not Yin without the Yang. Angels, demons, and spirits all exist together in unison to carry out their purpose creating a beautiful ecosystem of universal order. This is the sovereignty of God.

My son, do not despise the chastening of the LORD, Nor detest His correction; for whom the LORD loveth he correcteth; even as a father the son in whom he delighteth. | Proverbs 3:11

Trials, Tribulations and Testing

As we come into this new understanding of the hierarchy of Heavenly order and the way things work, our relationships with these lesser entities change, or at least our view of them does. As I look over my past I no longer feel like a victim to my environment or circumstances. I am now able to look back at all the hard times in life and thank God for them. I now see all of it as blessings from God rather than a curse. Admittedly while going through the tribulations sometimes you feel hopeless and you would give anything to exclude yourself from the situation. When we look back on it we can see the hand of God moving in every situation. There are some things that you cannot learn by simply taking someone's word for it. Sometimes we have to go through the trial and testing which is what produces character within us and is God's way of doing things. Trials are working out things within us that we cannot see. It is producing character and creating a natural empathy for the broken and those less fortunate. Going through fiery trials is the baptism of fire and faith alone is nothing, but faith when tested proves our faith and what we really believe in. Though crushed on every side, as we endure it produces an anointing within us just like the olive that is pressed produces precious oil. In this way so do our lives when laid down to the sanctification process of God.

Not only so, but we also glory in our sufferings, because we know that suffering produces perseverance; perseverance, character; and character, hope. And hope does not put us to shame, because God's love has been poured out into our hearts through the Holy Spirit, who has been given to us. | Romans 5:3-5

But doesn't the scripture say that God doesn't tempt anyone? Yes. Temptation and testing are two different things. When we face temptation it is usually something that allures our animalistic nature to some type of temporal satisfaction that usually doesn't produce life. The satisfaction is fleeting and if not checked early on can give birth to addictions and unhealthy habits. When we are tempted we are drawn away by our own lust and fleshly desires, but through every situation God has provided a way out. There is always a way of resistance and escape.

The testing of our faith is literally a test. We must prove what we believe by our actions. The way to pass each test is to respond with perfect love and perfect peace like Christ would. This is how we pass the test and are trusted with more, i.e. a greater anointing, favor etc. God the father is the author and finisher of our faith. He who started the good work within us is faithful and just to see us unto its completion. The way testing works with the hierarchy of Heaven is that spirits, angels or demons are loosed to carry out their assignment from God. It is not God himself that tempts us but he allows it and it is righteous. Responding with love and total trust in God is one of the greatest acts of worship. Though everything around us seems to be falling apart, though we have every reason to panic and freak out, we stand in faith knowing that the promises of God are Yes and Amen. Again, this is how we pass those tests and maintain our peace. Once we pass a test we may have to take a pop quiz sometime after just to make sure we still maintain the wisdom needed for spiritual growth unto maturity. If God finds us faithful with the small things he will be able to entrust to us the greater.

Part 1
The Sovereignty of God

Simon the Sorcerer and the Anointing

In Acts chapter 8 a man known as Simon the Sorcerer saw the apostles doing great and mighty deeds in the name of Christ. He saw them doing healings and when they would lay their hands upon people, those people would receive the baptism of the Holy Spirit. Simon being a well-studied man in magic asked the disciples if he could pay them to give him the ability that whoever he laid his hands on would receive the Holy Spirit as well. When Peter heard this he rebuked Simon saying

"MAY YOUR MONEY PERISH WITH YOU, BECAUSE YOU THOUGHT YOU COULD BUY THE GIFT OF GOD WITH MONEY! YOU HAVE NO PART OR SHARE IN THIS MINISTRY, BECAUSE YOUR HEART IS NOT RIGHT BEFORE GOD. REPENT OF THIS WICKEDNESS AND PRAY TO THE LORD IN THE HOPE THAT HE MAY FORGIVE YOU FOR HAVING SUCH A THOUGHT IN YOUR HEART. FOR I SEE THAT YOU ARE FULL OF BITTERNESS AND CAPTIVE TO SIN". | ACTS 8:20-23

Simon was rebuked for trying to buy the anointing. He was trying to buy what only comes through a life laid down to the sanctification process of God. Looking back over the lore and life of Simon the Sorcerer moving forward he later became one of the greatest magicians ever and to this day is venerated in many occult circles. Simon possessed spiritual powers that were given to him by lesser spirits. Legend says that years later Simon came back to town and challenged Peter to a duel to see who the greater magician was. As the crowds gathered to see the showdown, Simon said that he would be translated to heaven and actually began to levitate through the air with the help of demons. All the people were amazed and astonished at what a mighty magician he was. Legend goes on to say that when Peter and Paul saw this they both knelt to the ground,

Spirit Realm: Angels, Demons, Spirits and the Sovereignty of God

prayed to God and rebuked the demons. Upon doing this the demons left Simon as he fell to the ground and died.

This story represents the two paths. It represents human intellect vs God's way. It is the difference between black and white magick. Simon wanted to buy the anointing of God but it was not for sale. You cannot buy it with money; the only way to acquire the anointing is by a life laid down to the sanctification process and will of God.

(Benozzo di Lese di Sandro) (Italian, Florence ca. 1420–1497

Part 1
The Sovereignty of God

PART 2
ANGELS, SPIRITS AND DEMONS

A Spirit Passed Before My Face

IN A DREAM, IN A VISION OF THE NIGHT, WHEN DEEP SLEEP FALLETH UPON MEN, IN SLUMBERINGS UPON THE BED; THEN HE OPENETH THE EARS OF MEN, AND SEALETH THEIR INSTRUCTION. | JOB 33:16-17

It seems as if God waits until we are still before he can speak to us. Many of us are so busy throughout the week that through the hustle and bustle of life we can get caught up and barely even make time for God. This is why most of our revelations and downloads happen when the subconscious is unoccupied. Oftentimes when we are doing a task that requires only little thought it is easier to receive from Spirit. This often happens when we are driving a familiar commute, cutting the grass, jogging or taking a shower. When our mind is less occupied with sensory input it becomes easier for God to speak to us. This is why the practice of mindfulness and meditation is so significant in our lives. This is also the reason that God speaks so strongly to us during the dream state. As we lie on our beds for a night's rest, our bodies move through five stages of sleep. The order of the five stages is Delta, Theta, Alpha, Beta then Gamma. Each of these states allows our bodies to enter into an even deeper rest. As we progress through these sleep states, our brain releases DMT through our pineal gland or third eye. This is what allows us to dream.

Part 2
Angels, Spirits and Demons

James Tissot (French, 1836-1902)

The pineal gland produces melatonin, a serotonin-derived hormone which modulates sleep patterns in both circadian and seasonal cycles.

This release of DMT activates our imagination and opens us up to the dream world. The Bible is full of instances where God would wait until someone is asleep before He encountered them. There are many scriptures that tell us the power of the dream state. Many times God speaks through familiar signs and symbols in our dreams that we must search for the interpretation of at a later time. In Job chapter 4 Job speaks specifically about a spirit that approached him in the night. This spirit encounter sounds a lot like what some would call a ghost. I have personally had this same encounter with a similar spirit.

NOW A THING WAS SECRETLY BROUGHT TO ME, AND MINE EAR RECEIVED A LITTLE THEREOF. IN THOUGHTS FROM THE VISIONS OF THE NIGHT, WHEN DEEP SLEEP FALLETH ON MEN, FEAR CAME UPON ME, AND TREMBLING, WHICH MADE ALL MY BONES TO SHAKE. THEN A SPIRIT PASSED BEFORE MY FACE; THE HAIR OF MY FLESH STOOD UP: IT STOOD STILL, BUT I COULD NOT DISCERN THE FORM THEREOF: AN IMAGE WAS BEFORE MINE EYES, THERE WAS SILENCE, AND I HEARD A VOICE, SAYING, SHALL MORTAL MAN BE MORE JUST THAN GOD? SHALL A MAN BE MORE PURE THAN HIS MAKER? | JOB 4:12

In this encounter Job states that he was lying on his bed in the night when he saw a spirit hovering before him. This startled Job as he says that fear came upon him that caused his bones to shake. This is what we would call the chills as he goes on to state that the hair on his flesh stood up. It is interesting to note that when describing the spirit he says,

"IT STOOD STILL, BUT I COULD NOT DISCERN THE FORM THEREOF: AN IMAGE WAS BEFORE MINE EYES."

Part 2
Angels, Spirits and Demons

There are spirits who appear as a gas or mist. They are formless while continually changing shape. This is what many would call a ghost. The spirit did not just appear for Job to see to scare him, but to deliver a message. As we have stated, the word angel means messenger because they carry words back and forth from heaven to men. When these spirits arrive they bring with them feelings and emotions because they want to convey a message. The passage says that the spirit was silent but then Job heard a voice. This message was more than likely telepathic because spirits are able speak through vibrations and essences without using words. I have had a very similar experience with this type of spirit where it showed up to bring a message to me. It can be very frightening, especially when you wake up out of a deep sleep and the spirit is hovering before you. In order to receive the message intended for us, we must move past the fear.

Spirit Realm: Angels, Demons, Spirits and the Sovereignty of God

The Witching Hour

A voice from heaven to the youth of Great Britain, London, 1720

Encounters with the spirit realm seem to be more common during the witching hour. These encounters usually happen early in the morning around 3:00am which is known as the fourth watch. In the Book of Mark chapter 6 we read about an instance where the disciples were on a boat in the Sea of Galilee. While they were at sea they turned and saw Jesus walking on the water. This frightened them and they thought that it may have been a spirit or ghost. This is interesting to note because this experience was during the fourth watch. In Jewish mysticism it is believed that during this watch of the night, the veil between the spirit realm and our world is very thin. Many awaken during this fourth watch to get into intercessory prayer. The Jewish mystics believed that there was a special blessing upon those who were up praying during this watch. This is about 2-3 hours before the sun rises. In the Bible we see King David waking up and praying towards the East in the morning and Jews praying towards the East as well. It is believed that this is because they are praying towards the Holy city of Jerusalem but my studies have shown that this is a much older practice of Sun gazing and praying towards the Sun rise. There are sects of Buddhists and Hindus who awake during this time for meditation. They believe that there is less chatter in the ethers because the majority of the world is still asleep. From my personal experience I've seen more UFO and angelic activity in the early morning during the hours between 3-5am. Many who are into witchcraft honor this time as the witching hour and use it specifically for incantations and summoning spirits. In folklore, the witching hour or devil's hour is a time of morning associated with supernatural events. Creatures such as witches, demons and ghosts are thought to appear and to be at their most powerful. Black magic is thought to be most effective at this time as well. If you find yourself fully awake during the witching hour, try using the time to listen and pray to see if the lord is speaking to you.

Evil Spirits Sent From God

HE CAST UPON THEM THE FIERCENESS OF HIS ANGER, WRATH, AND INDIGNATION, AND TROUBLE, BY SENDING EVIL ANGELS AMONG THEM. | PSALM 78:49

In the book of 1 Samuel there is a story about David and King Saul. King Saul had it out for David and tried to kill him on many occasions because he was jealous of David's anointing. David was in the flow with God and everything he touched seemed to prosper with little effort. This made King Saul furious and because of his actions there was a spirit that was sent to torment Saul and deal treacherously with him. The only time that King Saul was able to find rest from the spirit was when David the psalmist played his harp for the king. If we look at the text a bit closer at the spirit that was upon Saul it actually says that it was an "evil spirit sent from God". This is one of the first cases that we see God sending forth evil spirits upon people in the scriptures.

David och Saul (1878) målad av Ernst Josephson

THEN SAMUEL TOOK THE HORN OF OIL, AND ANOINTED HIM IN THE MIDST OF HIS BRETHREN: AND THE SPIRIT OF THE LORD CAME UPON DAVID FROM THAT DAY FORWARD. SO SAMUEL ROSE UP, AND WENT TO RAMAH.
BUT THE SPIRIT OF THE LORD DEPARTED FROM SAUL, AND AN EVIL SPIRIT FROM THE LORD TROUBLED HIM.
AND SAUL'S SERVANTS SAID UNTO HIM, BEHOLD NOW, AN EVIL SPIRIT FROM GOD TROUBLETH THEE. | 1 SAMUEL 16:13-15

Part 2
Angels, Spirits and Demons

Here is another example in **Judges 9:23 Then God sent an evil spirit between Abimelech and the men of Shechem; and the men of Shechem dealt treacherously with Abimelech**

The Angel of The Lord

On several occasions in the Bible God sent forth His destroying angel known in scripture as "The Angel of The Lord". This angel seemed to play a huge part in destruction and retribution from God. On several occasions he was sent to destroy hundreds of thousands of people. Many times during his appearance he is noted for having a flaming sword. He appears throughout the entirety of the Bible bringing messages and causing destruction. He seems to work as the "right hand of the Lord" and even appears at the tomb of Jesus to roll the stone away. Many speculate that he was the death angel that destroyed Egypt and killed all the first born children of Egyptians. It is also believed that He is the bodily angelic manifestation of Yahweh Himself, or at least a piece of Him.

Spirits Don't Die

When understanding how spirits work and operate, we must realize that spirits don't die like humans do. Though the flesh may fade the spirit is eternal. We are eternal beings experiencing time and eternity slowed down. The same spirits that Moses fought against are still here in the Earth today. Pharaoh has passed and is long gone, but the same spirits that were influencing his decisions are here today. The following portion of scripture has been a mystery in times past, and if not read in proper context one may simply skim over such a great truth presented by Jesus.

THE QUEEN OF THE SOUTH SHALL RISE UP IN THE JUDGMENT WITH THIS GENERATION, AND SHALL CONDEMN IT: FOR SHE CAME FROM THE UTTERMOST PARTS OF THE EARTH TO HEAR THE WISDOM OF SOLOMON; AND, BEHOLD, A GREATER THAN SOLOMON *IS* HERE.

WHEN THE UNCLEAN SPIRIT IS GONE OUT OF A MAN, HE WALKETH THROUGH DRY PLACES, SEEKING REST, AND FINDETH NONE.
THEN HE SAITH, I WILL RETURN INTO MY HOUSE FROM WHENCE I CAME OUT; AND WHEN HE IS COME, HE FINDETH *IT* EMPTY, SWEPT, AND GARNISHED.

THEN GOETH HE, AND TAKETH WITH HIMSELF SEVEN OTHER SPIRITS MORE WICKED THAN HIMSELF, AND THEY ENTER IN AND DWELL THERE: AND THE LAST *STATE* OF THAT MAN IS WORSE THAN THE FIRST. EVEN SO SHALL IT BE ALSO UNTO THIS WICKED GENERATION. | MATTHEW 12:42-45

Jesus is letting us know that the spirit that was behind the Queen of the South (Queen Sheba) would return to the Earth to persecute and condemn their generation. This lets us know that even though Queen Sheba has passed on that the influencing spirits are still here or would be returning soon.

Her plan that was devised while she was here was to challenge King Solomon to make a mockery of his wisdom and his devotion to Yahweh. To execute this, she planned to meet with Solomon and came up with hard questions and accusations that she knew he could never answer. She gathered all of her people and met with Solomon. When it was time for the debate Solomon answered all of her questions and nothing was too hard for him. She was amazed and overwhelmed with the wisdom and knowledge that Solomon possessed so much so that the evil accusing spirit left her.

Part 2
Angels, Spirits and Demons

St. Francis Borgia Helping a Dying Impenitent circa 1788

This is the spirit that Jesus said would return to condemn the generation. This is mainly the spirit of accusation and debate that we see behind many of the professors in colleges around the world. They devise hard questions to try and confuse young people and talk them out of their faith in God and into logic and reason. Many times their pursuit stems from a deep hurt or anger that they hold towards God and the church. The interesting thing that we learn from the interaction between Solomon and Sheba is that he was able to "cast out" her evil spirit simply with truth. The powerful thing about this is that we have the same ability to do this as well simply through our conversations. This is why Paul says Let your speech be always with grace, seasoned with salt, that ye may know how ye ought to answer every man. | Colossians 4:6

These demonic entities gain access to a person's life by agreeing with their lie or half-truth. In 2 Corinthians 10:3 the apostle Paul says

For though we walk in the flesh, we do not war after the flesh:

For the weapons of our warfare *are* not carnal, but mighty through God to the pulling down of strong holds;

Casting down imaginations, and every high thing that exalteth itself against the knowledge of God, and bringing into captivity every thought to the obedience of Christ.

The imaginations mentioned here speak of how unclean spirits are able to influence humans.

The Bible describes spiritual strongholds when referring to demonic possession. These strongholds are simply

Part 2
Angels, Spirits and Demons

thought-forms and ideas contrary to the will of God for your life, also known as ungodly beliefs. This is also an entryway for demonic possession. Agreeing with the terms and ideas that are not for your highest good gives legal contract for these entities to take residence within your auric field. That's why Jesus says you shall know the truth and the truth shall make you free. These ungodly beliefs cause preconceived notions and we begin to see things not as though they are but as we are. This also comes up in people with Post-Traumatic Stress Disorder and those who have had relationship trauma or trust issues. Because of past experiences, they may not trust a member from the opposite sex again. These beliefs can hinder our relationships moving forward and distort our view and why they are in our lives. The way to break free from these ideas is to know the truth of what God says about us.

People are fighting their own personal battles and a person who is sensitive to the Holy Spirit can use the gift of discernment to extend grace to a person battling with identity issues from ungodly beliefs. The power of life and death are in the tongue and we as sons and daughters of God have the power to bind and loose on Earth as it is in heaven. One of the easiest yet most effective things that we can do is to work with God through conversation to offer hope and encouragement to those who are lost.

FOR WE WRESTLE NOT AGAINST FLESH AND BLOOD, BUT AGAINST PRINCIPALITIES, AGAINST POWERS, AGAINST THE RULERS OF THE DARKNESS OF THIS WORLD, AGAINST SPIRITUAL WICKEDNESS IN HIGH PLACES. | EPHESIANS 6:12

Spirit Realm: Angels, Demons, Spirits and the Sovereignty of God

Fallen Angels

Illustration 11 of Edgar Allan Poe's Raven Gustave Doré (1832–1883)

When understanding fallen angels within the Bible we must consider Genesis Chapter 6. Genesis 6:4 reads; There were giants in the earth in those days; and also after that, when the sons of God came in unto the daughters of men, and they bore *children* to them, the same *became* mighty men which *were* of old, men of renown. Dissecting this verse we see that the Bible uses the term "Sons of God" ("Bene ha Elohim") which is continually used when speaking about the angels. The text says that the sons of God or angels "came into" (implying sexual union) the daughters of men and bore giants or mighty men, men of renown. This notion implies that the angels looked down from their heavenly habitat and saw women on the earth with such beauty that they could not control themselves. They left heaven and came down to mate with women, which was forbidden. These women bore children from these angels and the children were believed to be angel / human hybrids or giants known as the Nephilim. When the

Part 2
Angels, Spirits and Demons

angels tried to ascend back into heaven God forbade them because they were not to defile themselves with women. God then punishes them by sending them into hell or the deep parts of the earth to be restrained in chain of darkness until judgement day where they will be judged by Yahweh and the saints of God. Hence the scripture says;

DO YOU NOT KNOW THAT WE WILL JUDGE ANGELS?

| 1 CORINTHIANS 6:3

Now the children of the fallen angels and women were believed to be evil. The Book of Enoch says that they were eating people and teaching mankind all types of wickedness. It was also said that the children were so big that most of the mothers died in labor. The reason that God sent the deluge or flood of Noah to wipe the Nephilim off of the face of the earth was because of their wickedness and how much of an influence they had over mankind. God sent forth a spirit upon them to cause them to be at war with one another and this is also believed to be where the Wars of the Titans arose from as well as many of the Greek and Egyptian stories. When a Nephilim died, God forbid their spirit from entering heaven and yet they were not to be on earth either so God left them stuck between the realms longing for rest and finding none. They now torment and influence mankind from the ethers. They still long to have a body and get to feel the sensations of their past life as long as they have a human host. When they entice men to murder, rob or commit any type of wickedness on their earth, they get to feel that pleasure. They miss their pervious form and the delicacies of humanity. The souls of the Nephilim are what we now consider a sect of evil spirits. This is the doctrine according to the book of Enoch that is also reiterated throughout the scriptures. Enoch was once held in high regard by the early church but Constantine and the council of Nicaea removed many of the books that were once within the Bible. The book of Jude almost did not make the cut because it contains a direct prophecy quoted from the Book of Enoch saying;

AND ENOCH ALSO, THE SEVENTH FROM ADAM, PROPHESIED OF THESE, SAYING, BEHOLD, THE LORD COMETH WITH TEN THOUSANDS OF HIS SAINTS, TO EXECUTE JUDGMENT UPON ALL, AND TO CONVINCE ALL THAT ARE UNGODLY AMONG THEM OF ALL THEIR UNGODLY DEEDS WHICH THEY HAVE UNGODLY COMMITTED, AND OF ALL THEIR HARD *SPEECHES* WHICH UNGODLY SINNERS HAVE SPOKEN AGAINST HIM. | JUDE 1:15

The book of second peter was also up for debate because it also gives and obscure reference to the angels that left their abode:

FOR IF GOD SPARED NOT THE ANGELS THAT SINNED, BUT CAST *THEM* DOWN TO HELL, AND DELIVERED *THEM* INTO CHAINS OF DARKNESS, TO BE RESERVED UNTO JUDGMENT; AND SPARED NOT THE OLD WORLD, BUT SAVED NOAH THE EIGHTH *PERSON*, A PREACHER OF RIGHTEOUSNESS, BRINGING IN THE FLOOD UPON THE WORLD OF THE UNGODLY;

| 2 PETER 2:4-5

Spirituality and Hair

In 1 Corinthians 11 Paul is speaking on proper ways to pray and says that a woman should not pray with her head uncovered. It goes on to say that a woman should have power over her own head and to cover it before she prays because of the angels. It says that a woman's hair is her glory and yet the beauty of the hair is what caused the angels to sin. Hair is very powerful and symbolic within the scriptures. The Native Americans believed that their hair was an extension of their nervous system and made them more alert and intuitive. There were even studies performed that showed how natives would be awakened out of a deep slumber when someone was close by trying to cause them harm. Once they shaved their head the results were not the same. It is believed that they lost their keen intuition once their hair was cut. We read in the story of Samson in the Bible that his power was literally within his hair. When his head was shaved, he lost his power and uniqueness and became like every other man. It is similar to the root system of a tree that digs deep within the earth to communicate with other trees and the plant life around it. Our hair is believed to act as our roots that extend out of our nervous system become as an antenna to communicate with heaven and tune into frequencies and energy. Paul says that if a woman pray with her head uncovered it would be better for her to be shaven bald because as she prays the angels would notice it and her hair may entice them once again. This is why the custom is still around today for Jewish women, Catholic nuns and Muslim ladies all to wear head coverings over their heads. This tradition is also still practiced in the black churches in the south with women wearing large fancy hats during Sunday service.

With the book of Enoch filling so many holes in Biblical doctrine why would they take it out? Why would they call it heretical or uninspired? To understand this we must look at what it exposes. When referring to spirits and fallen angels, Enoch says that their goal is to entice those in high positions. These positions are places of power within the Earth such as the government, educational, medical, entertainment and religious systems. The deities of old demanded worship and in exchange they would give power to those who bowed a knee. As silly as ancient culture is to many in the western world, these gods of old are still being worshipped under different names and titles yet their customs, rituals and sacrifices are still being kept even today. They are honored still by sacrifice, holidays and wickedness upon the Earth and exchange their glory for power, renown and influence. These truths are still maintained by many in the mystery schools and those initiated into secret societies and fraternities.

Sleep Paralysis and Shadow People

Ephialtes, from the 1863 edition of Collin de Plancy's Dictionnaire infernal

When I was around four years old I can still remember the night that I awoke in my bed to a terrible feeling of the presence of two shadow beings lying on each side of me.

Part 2
Angels, Spirits and Demons

The shadows were pinning me down to the bed. I was afraid and did not know what to do. I don't know if I couldn't speak or if I was just too afraid to for fear that they would know that I was awake. I was paralyzed with fear. Around that same time in my life, I woke up after midnight and walked through the house and walked into my mom's room. There was a clothes basket right past the doorway and the room was dark and in the basket were two red glowing eyes looking at me. Throughout my childhood, my friends and I were always trying to scare ourselves by hiding from each other and jumping out, telling ghost stories or watching scary movies. Pretty typical stuff, but throughout my whole childhood it tortured me. Every time I turned the light off I was scared, but the even scarier part was when I closed my eyes. Most nights I had nightmares. I had them so often that I learned how to lucid dream to get out of them. Every time I wanted to wake up I would just suffocate myself in the dream, cut my own throat, drown myself, or jump head first into a rock to kill myself or break my neck. It worked every time. I always woke up out of the nightmares when I did this. The scariest dreams were when I was trying to go to sleep and looking around at my room and I didn't know that I had fallen asleep. In my dream I would still be lying there in bed looking around my room and either a demon would come walking in my room, or one would be on top of me and I couldn't move. This phenomenon was quite different than the experience that I had as a child with the shadow beings lying on my chest. The Lord didn't give us a spirit of fear, but of love and a sound mind. I just hadn't learned this yet.

I learned through my studies and personal experiences with these entities that they are sent to try and place fear into the hearts and minds of those who are destined to do mighty things for the light. Most of the time people have encounters with these beings when they are children. These beings come to try and rob them of their innocence. Many people I know who have had these encounters end up doing great exploits serving humanity and spreading love in their adult lives. It seems as if they are marked at an early age by some type of dark force to try and keep them away from pursuing anything spiritual. People call these beings witches, shadow people and even report seeing silhouettes of men standing in their room wearing a top hat and trenchcoat. Others have named this the old hag syndrome speaking about experiences where they wake up out of a dead sleep and cannot move and an old woman is laying on top of them screaming. Scientifically and clinically it is said that sleep paralysis is where a person wakes up consciously and even opens their eyes but their body is still asleep resulting in a paralyzing stasis of fear. That could be true, but why are there usually shadow beings, demons, imps and creatures in a person's room when this is taking place? My belief is that this is something that is supernatural in nature and may be even feeding off of people's energy while they are asleep. Waking up in the middle of the night not being able to move or speak is definitely terrifying but having a scary entity present doesn't help the situation. If it is just because we are in alpha sleep why isn't it a pink elephant that appears? Why isn't it something lovely and beautiful that we often encounter in the dream state? Why is it always some grotesque looking entity that is present when sleep paralysis occurs?

Part 2
Angels, Spirits and Demons

London, British Library, MS Royal 2 B VII, f. 227v, SE England, c. 1310-1320

Spirit Realm: Angels, Demons, Spirits and the Sovereignty of God

PART 3
FAMILIAR SPIRITS AND CHANNELING

Ventriloquist / Channeling

Histoires prodigieuses; Histoire d'un prestre... WMS 136

Part 3
Familiar Spirits and Channeling

AND IT CAME TO PASS, AS WE WENT TO PRAYER, A CERTAIN DAMSEL POSSESSED WITH A SPIRIT OF DIVINATION MET US, WHICH BROUGHT HER MASTERS MUCH GAIN BY SOOTHSAYING: THE SAME FOLLOWED PAUL AND US, AND CRIED, SAYING, THESE MEN ARE THE SERVANTS OF THE MOST HIGH GOD, WHICH SHEW UNTO US THE WAY OF SALVATION. AND THIS DID SHE MANY DAYS. BUT PAUL, BEING GRIEVED, TURNED AND SAID TO THE SPIRIT, I COMMAND THEE IN THE NAME OF JESUS CHRIST TO COME OUT OF HER. AND HE CAME OUT THE SAME HOUR... | ACTS 16:16-18

The scripture goes on to tell us that once this spirit was cast out of her that she lost her "power" to predict the future and tell fortunes. But let's look a little closer at the translation of the spirit referenced here. Verse 16 says that that it is the spirit of divination. Divination is a practice used in many cultures and traditions including the Hebraic tradition, yet, divination is not a "spirit". It is only when we go into the Latin word used that we are able to gain insight on what is really being conveyed here. The Greek word is Puthone or Python and is actually referred to as the Greek God Pythone.

In Greek mythology, Python was the serpent, sometimes represented as a dragon, living at the center of the earth, believed by the ancient Greeks to be at Delphi. This is considered in Biblical terms to be a familiar spirit. The Hebrew translation and definition of familiar spirit brings us to two notable concepts. The first is Genies or Djinns which are spirits that are trapped within jars or magical lamps that can be caught and used to gain insight about the future or grant wishes. The second part of the word familiar spirit is the same meaning for the Greek word ventriloquist, which is what the ancient Greeks called themselves who channeled the spirit of Pythone. Oftentimes the ventriloquist oracles of Delphi would get themselves intoxicated with gasses that were extruding from the caves in Delphi. It was found that ethane, methane, and ethylene were in the water near the Oracle. The euphoric effects of ethylene, which had been used as anesthesia in the last century allowed them to channel deeper parts of their psyche and enter hypnotic states. Just as a modern ventriloquist would use a puppet to convey a message, channeling is liken to the human being the puppet allowing their bodies to be used as a vessel to relay information from the spirits in the ethers.

Puthon
poo'-thone
Ventriloquist
Word Origin and History for ventriloquist

1650s, from *Ventriloquists in ancient Greece were Pythones, a reference to the Delphic Oracle.*

The Oracle of Delphi Entranced, by Heinrich Leutemann (1824–1905).

I believe there is a right way and a wrong way of doing things and we were created to be in natural communion with God by the way of our spiritual abilities. Channeling is another way that we communicate with God and other beings. With channeling in mind, we can sit in stillness and meditate and receive messages directly from God for our own lives and for those around us. We can literally channel the Father's heart and get beautiful downloads of inspiration directly from heaven. Many people who have tapped into their spiritual abilities have used their gifts to channel different entities other than God or those of the heavenly realms. Some channel ghosts or the spirits of passed loved ones. Many try and channel dead celebrities such as Michael Jackson or Hitler and others open themselves up to communicate with any spirit out there in the ethers that want to communicate. This is probably by far the easiest way to become demonically possessed by unclean or familiar spirits. Not every spirit is enlightened just because they are on the other side.

We are fearfully and wonderfully made and our anatomy is embedded with ways to receive energy and influences from outside sources. Our pineal gland or third eye acts as a spiritual eye, allowing us to see into the spirit realm and discern the spirits thereof. Our hair is an extension of our central nervous system and acts as an antenna to pick up on frequencies. Our skin can also let us know when spirits are around or trying to communicate in the form of chills or goosebumps. Some believe that the strong ringing in the ears heard by many when they are alone allows for us to naturally get into trance state and have ecstatic spiritual experiences such as Astral Projection and Time Travel. These are but just a few ways that we communicate with God and the angelic powers that be.

In the scriptures we are forbidden to consult with familiar spirits. These are lower level entities or gods that oftentimes masquerade as benevolent beings, but are mischievous and use trickery to deceive. They are dishonest and lead their subject into possession. The Bible describes spiritual strongholds when referring to demonic possession. As mentioned earlier, these strongholds are simply thought-forms and ideas contrary to the will of God for your life. These are also known as ungodly beliefs. This is also an entryway for demonic possession. Agreeing with the terms and ideas that are not for your highest good gives legal contract for these entities to take residence within your auric field. We must use discernment to test the spirits to see their intention and find out their agenda. Now this is not the case with angelic contact or receiving messages from the Holy Spirit. We are shown throughout scriptures that angels and other beings were sent by Yahweh to bring messages to men on earth. This is not to negate spirit contact as a whole, but simply to understand which spirits we are entertaining.

Socrates the father of Philosophy in Greek antiquity claimed to have been entertained by the spirit of a Daemon. A Daemon is a kind of divine spirit, oracle, or "sign," that takes the form of an inner voice or non-vocal nudge. This Daemon spoke with him regularly in the form of a voice about some of his mistakes. It seems as if this inner voice was maybe his conscience or what believers call the Holy Spirt. The Bible says that one of the main roles of the Holy Spirit is to work with our conscience convicting the world of sin.

Nikolai Tesla believed that he was in contact with extraterrestrial alien intelligence. While tracking thunderstorms, Nikolai claimed that he received messages that were not from earth in the forms of beeps. In February of 1901, Tesla proclaimed his belief in aliens in an article titled "Talking with the Planets". Through his inventions, Nikolai believed that he was able to communicate with the off world entities. Many of his later

Part 3
Familiar Spirits and Channeling

writings contained diagrams of what appeared to be UFOs and claimed that through harnessing electricity that one could cause these objects to levitate.

William Blake Satan Going Forth from the Presence of the Lord, and Job's Charity 1825

Reincarnation

What does the Bible say about reincarnation? Should Christians believe in it? Where do we go when we die? Better yet, where were we before we incarnated into this realm of existence? For many evangelical Christians the idea of reincarnation seems preposterous and anti-Biblical, but there are some obscure verses within the scriptures that give notion that souls or spirits of the deceased may come back to earth in other forms. On the topic of spirits, we must understand that people die and bodies are destroyed but the spirit is eternal. During the ministry of Jesus, many people were speaking among themselves as to who this miracle working man was. Some said Elijah and others said Jeremiah or one of the prophets. This gives us the notion that the ancients Jews believed that spirits would reincarnate into other vessels.

There was also a time when Jesus's disciples were speaking to him about John the Baptist and asking who he really was and Jesus answered "And if you care to accept it, he himself is Elijah, who was to come". There is much debate whether he was literally Elijah in the flesh or if he was operating under the spirit and office of Elijah. It seems that the majority of Christendom believes that once we die we are immediately translated into the presence of God. This is because Paul stated that to be absent from the body is to be present with the Lord. The Bible speaks about other places that souls enter into once they are done with their life here on earth. The Apocrypha is 14 books that were removed from the King James Bible that were originally a part of it. Within the Apocrypha are details about the journey that souls must undergo once they leave the body. These books were taken out of the Bible for various doctrinal reasons.

Part 3
Familiar Spirits and Channeling

God's answer to Job, Adriaen Collaert, after Jan van der Straet, 1587 –1591

I believe Earth to be a training ground with many lessons, testings and experiences for eternity. Many people believe that we will be given roles in the age to come. What if that age is already here and when we cross over to the other side we face the judgement seat of Christ and are given roles according to our performance here on Earth? For some, that could be reincarnating here again to retake the parts of the tests that they failed. Others who have learned their lessons are possibly welcomed with a "Well done thy good and faithful servant" receive their according rewards / crowns and take their rightful place in the kingdom. Maybe they get to join the great cloud of witnesses and teach from the other side. Maybe they are to judge angels and are given heavenly duties or maybe they are stuck in the ethers in-between on a loop repeating the same mistakes over and over until they serve out that sentence. Although I do not believe in eternal torments any longer, the apocalypse of Peter goes into great detail about paying for our sins on the other side. Much like the concept of hell, which was inspired by Dante's Inferno, Peter shares about how humans will be tormented by demons on the other side according to their sins and the wickedness that they committed. For example, those who have raped on Earth will in turn be raped by the spirits that be.

Communing With The Dead

In Matthew 17:2 we read about Jesus upon the mount of transfiguration meeting with elder champions of the faith, Moses and Elijah. Jesus's garments and face transformed into their light body form radiating with a bright white light and this was witnessed by not only by Saint Peter but also by James and John. This was the first time that someone was privy to be a part of what Jesus practiced during his prayer time when he would draw away for hours on end to pray. We find that he wasn't simply praying for people or going over a prayer list but actually communing with the Father and meeting the saints and prophets of old. To fully understand this we must look to the East. Many religious and spiritual traditions believe that our ancestors and spiritual teachers continue to teach us from beyond the grave. This isn't that far outside of Christian thinking. True Christianity has its origins in eastern thought. There are verses about ghosts as well as stories about conjuring up the dead that actually took place in the Bible.

Part 3
Familiar Spirits and Channeling

James Tissot (French, 1836-1902). The Transfiguration (La transfiguration), 1886-1896

In 1 Samuel 28, King Saul conjured up the spirit of Samuel which came forth during a séance to speak with King Saul. Connecting with the spirits of the deceased is becoming more and more accepted within many Christian circles in the West. Many Christians in recent years have reported seeing their elders who have since passed into eternity meeting with them face to face as apparitions in hotel rooms and even in dreams and visions in the night.

Scapegoat

There are many examples of people stepping out of the social norm and losing everything that they worked hard to build. For example, in 2018 Rosanne Barr's show made a comeback after 20 years. The show debuted in the number one spot and the media was buzzing about it. During its height, she woke up in the middle of the night supposedly out of an Ambien and alcohol induced sleep and tweeted what many perceived to be a racist slur about former President Obama's senior advisor Valerie Jarrett. When Roseanne woke up the next morning her tweet had made headlines and she soon after got a call from ABC letting her know that her Services were no longer needed. Roseanne Barr was fired from her own show. Roseanne says that the Tweet was meant to be a political tweet but everyone disagreed and said that it came off racist. There is this weird thing inside of humans that loves to see people rise to power and fame and then fall flat on their faces to join the rest of society at the bottom. We've also seen this with Logan Paul, the famous YouTuber who took a trip to Aokigahara to visit Japan's famous suicide forest. He went there to Vlog and camp out and maybe shoot a creepy video but ended up finding a dead body hanging from one of the trees deep inside of the forest. He filmed the body and turned his vlog into somewhat of a PSA for suicide prevention but as soon as the upload went public there was immediate backlash. YouTube cut his earnings in

Part 3
Familiar Spirits and Channeling

half and many brands that he was affiliated with immediately pulled out and social media went crazy and everyone had something to say about Logan and his despicable act. Logan Paul comes off as very obnoxious and annoying and many adults can't stand him but he has been a big hit with children and teenagers. People almost seemed to be waiting for Logan to fall from grace and lose everything that he had worked so hard to build. There was a lot of anticipation for his demise and the people finally got what they wanted. All the other YouTubers and bloggers went in on Logan about why he's a bad person, why he should be banned from YouTube and how he should never be forgiven. The people rejoiced. There are countless other stories where celebrities and historical figures rise to power and then fall from grace and the people love it. Oftentimes the people who fall are destroyed by the same ones who lifted them up to that platform to begin with. They show their love, give support, adorning them with adoration but the moment they say or do something outside of what the people are used to or believe they are quickly made an example. Jesus was killed by his own people, the same people whom he came to save. The same happened with Martin Luther King, JFK, John Lennon and Malcolm X. Sometimes these people are assassinated, but in this information age that we're now in, it's done socially and digitally just like in the case of Alex Jones. Alex Jones took his free speech a little bit too far with crazy conspiracy theories. These theories carried a little bit too much influence over his audience. He said some things that made a lot of people mad and ended up getting deplatformed from all of the major social media outlets, email providers and other private owned companies that are used to distribute content. With the push of a button they deleted all of his uploads. Affiliates and advertisers backed out and with the push of a button the majority of his existence outside of his personal website was gone. Again, when this happened the people

68

rejoiced. I read a book when I was younger in school called The Whipping Boy and it was about this beggar kid who was made to stand in proxy to receive the punishment of a young prince to be. Since he was royalty no one would lay a hand on him so they would bring in The Whipping Boy in to whip him and give him the punishment that belonged to the prince. This is also apparent in the story of Christ where the people deserve to be punished for their sins but Christ goes to the cross and takes their punishment upon himself. This is also shown in the Old Testament in the form of the scapegoat, as well as the sacrificial lamb. Most people do not want to take responsibility for their own actions, but will stand up immediately to blame others for their own mistakes and wrongdoings. Humanity has a fascination with murder, floggings and other people's misery.

Part 3
Familiar Spirits and Channeling

Sending Out the Scapegoat, by William James Webb (1830—1904)

After exhaustive research I have found that what we see going on within many of the channeling circles is not true spirit channeling at all. Many have tapped into the deeper parts of their own psyche and use channeling as a scapegoat to say how they really feel when fear of the repercussions and ridicule of their peers keeps them from being honest. This form of channeling places the blame on whatever "spirit" or "character" is said to be delivering the message. Many people have felt a certain way for some time but have been too afraid to voice their own opinion. The individual receives a boost of confidence when they let the character speak. In ventriloquism we see mostly shy introverted people receive a huge boost of courage and

70

find the ability to say things that they would never say to a person as themselves, even though inwardly they would love to. While channeling, the individual's voice may change so that they take on the persona of another character. Their movements and facial expressions can change as well.

Everyone is born with supernatural abilities that become dormant if not cultivated and utilized from a young age. We are seeing an emergence in these abilities as people are awakening all across the globe about their reality and who they really are. Some people may use ESP (Extra Sensory Perception), empathy or their intuition to be able to pick up on things in or around an individual. This is something that everyone is capable of and is referenced within the Bible as the discernment of spirits. Many have experienced this since childhood and were just told that they have an overactive imagination. In many cases, children are drugged to stop messages and feelings from coming through from the ethers with the use of Ritalin. This is why we feel it is important to get the information out on this subject matter. With global awakening now in full swing, many are now looking to harness their psychic abilities. This fits in with the subject matter because with each one of these God given abilities comes a scapegoat. With each one there is always someone or something to lay the blame on. For the psychic, it's the crystal ball. For the tarot reader, it's the cards. For the channeler or medium, it is the spirit. For those who practice spiritual giftings in the church, it's God. There is always a way out, and someone to lay the blame on just in case you are wrong or miss the mark. I am convinced that the knowledge and inspiration that comes through these channelings and readings could come to the practitioner without the use of the scapegoat. It is the power of the ritual that creates a safe space or divine essence to speak while many are already inspired.

Part 3
Familiar Spirits and Channeling

Spirit Realm: Angels, Demons, Spirits and the Sovereignty of God

PART 4
BEINGS OF LIGHT

Painting "The Sheperds and the angel" (1879) by Carl Bloch.

Angels appear in many forms. Sometimes the appearance of specific angelic forces are associated with light or "light beings". There are several key scriptures for us to examine with the first being Enoch Chapter 17:1-2 which states

Part 4
Beings of Light

AND THEY TOOK AND BROUGHT ME TO A PLACE IN WHICH THOSE WHO WERE THERE WERE LIKE FLAMING FIRE, AND, WHEN THEY WISHED, THEY APPEARED AS MEN.

Enoch explains that the angels appeared as a flaming fire, but if they wished they were able to take on bodies for themselves to present themselves to men. This is usually what happens when angels come to earth to converse with men. As fire they are able to travel faster than the speed of light. This is also known as "the twinkling of an eye". Matter is not able to travel that fast. For matter to appear, it must be slowed down and essentially subject itself to time. Another scripture that describes particular angels as fire or light is Psalm 104:3 which says

WHO LAYETH THE BEAMS OF HIS CHAMBERS IN THE WATERS: WHO MAKETH THE CLOUDS HIS CHARIOT: WHO WALKETH UPON THE WINGS OF THE WIND: WHO MAKETH HIS ANGELS SPIRITS; HIS MINISTERS A FLAMING FIRE.

This is also reiterated in the New Testament in Hebrews Chapter 1:14. Enoch goes on to explain that the angelic beings are made out of the fire and the essence of God. The Bible also states that our God is an all-consuming fire, hence the cloud by day and fire by night that the Israelites followed in the wilderness. The Bible says in 1 John1:5 that God actually IS light and in Him there is not darkness. Light exists as a vibrational frequency that can be measured and seen. This is why the Hebrews declare "Hear O Israel, The LORD is ONE". God is in ALL and through ALL and nothing exists that can claim itself that is not vibration or light. God is literally in everything. Life is energy, movement and growth and such is the Kingdom of God. There are many different spectrums and colors of light as depicted in the rainbow, and there are angels and beings that vibrate on different light frequencies in which they also travel.

Spirit Realm: Angels, Demons, Spirits and the Sovereignty of God

The Seraphim are a part of the angelic order and Hierarchy of God and their name literally translates to "The Fiery Ones".

In Judges 13:20 there is a story about when Manoah meets with an angel of the Lord. The angel actually leaves their presence and ascends into heaven by entering into a flame of fire that Manoah built as a burnt offering to God. The ancients believed that fire was holy itself and offered it up to God as a sacrifice. They believed that the smoke carried their prayers up to heaven.

Manoah and his Wife. Illustration for Bible Picture Book (SPCK, c 1880).

Part 4
Beings of Light

Satan: An Angel of Light?

In this next portion I would like to address a fear and caution that I have heard from many church goers concerning angels of light. In the church there is an overwhelming fascination with demons and the demonic. People love to share their stories. When it comes to angels, there is a bit of disbelief and many do not believe that angelic contact is possible. One of the cautions I've heard that pushes this disbelief is "You'd better be careful because even Satan and his demons can appear as an angel of light". There is such a fear of being deceived that many stray away from expecting angelic experiences and contact. The verse that many quote is 2 Corinthians 11:14 which says

AND NO MARVEL; FOR SATAN HIMSELF IS TRANSFORMED INTO AN ANGEL OF LIGHT. THEREFORE IT IS NO GREAT THING IF HIS MINISTERS ALSO BE TRANSFORMED AS THE MINISTERS OF RIGHTEOUSNESS.

Out of context this scripture is somewhat of a warning about demons appearing to people pretending to be beautiful angels. Another scripture even says not to believe any other doctrine even if an angel brings it to you. This has people believing that most of the encounters we have with the angelic are actually demons, but if we examine this scripture closer and in proper context we can see that this is not the case. 2 Corinthians 11 is not warning us about Satan or demons appearing as beautiful angelic beings. In context the text says that these angels or messengers spoken of here are actually people. More specifically, people pretending to be ministers of God i.e. pastors, preachers, teachers, priest etc. This is the problem with taking scriptures out of context and building doctrine and theology around them, which sadly seems to be the majority of western Christianity.

The context of the text reads
For such *are* false apostles, deceitful workers, transforming themselves into the apostles of Christ.

AND NO MARVEL; FOR SATAN HIMSELF IS TRANSFORMED INTO AN ANGEL OF LIGHT. THEREFORE *IT IS* NO GREAT THING IF HIS MINISTERS ALSO BE TRANSFORMED AS THE MINISTERS OF RIGHTEOUSNESS; WHOSE END SHALL BE ACCORDING TO THEIR WORKS. | 2 CORINTHIANS 11:13-15

As we read this particular scripture in context we see that it is not talking about angels as in angelic light beings, but actually false prophets and apostles. As discussed earlier, the word angel translates to "messenger". Paul here is simply echoing Jesus

BEWARE OF FALSE PROPHETS, WHICH COME TO YOU IN SHEEP'S CLOTHING, BUT INWARDLY THEY ARE RAVENING WOLVES. | MATTHEW 7:15

Should we be afraid of angelic contact? Not at all! We most certainly should test all spirits to see whether they be of Christ and for our greater good. There are entities on the other side that want to cause humans harm and lead us down an egoic path of deception, but there are even more that are for us that actually exist to aid humanity. I have been on both sides of this spectrum and it is only right that we caution people seeking encounters, but it is also our duty to encourage exploration.

Part 4
Beings of Light

Angelic Contact

Collected stories" by A.S. Pushkin published in 18xx, Russia

Have you ever had an encounter with an angel? How about more than once? Have you ever experienced a divine miracle? Angelic encounters are possible but they shouldn't end there. After these encounters, what was the message that was communicated with you? Take the message and run with it. The apostle Paul did this and went on to write the majority of the New Testament. As beautiful and awe

78

inspiring as these types of supernatural encounters are, I feel like people in the West just want more and more. They seem to never be satisfied or content. They always want more. This is especially what I have seen in the charismatic circles in Christianity. I have been a part of countless Church services and meetings where people were begging God in prayer for a supernatural encounter for hours and then... suddenly... something happens. A mighty rushing wind blows through the place and the Spirit of the Lord shows up so strong that everyone is on the floor stuck with their faces in the carpet grieving over their sin because of the weighty presence of God. I've had amazing encounters like this in a church of full of hundreds of people, but also even alone in my own prayer closet. I could talk for hours about these beautiful encounters (and I do on the TruthSeekah Podcast) and I'm sure you could too, but what is the end goal? How many supernatural encounters with God do you need? How many angelic encounters are you looking for? Often in the Bible they just needed one encounter. They received their message or their vision and then ran with it. We see the same thing with encounters with Jesus. People come face to face with him and he changes their life and then they're off, ready to share with the whole world the wonderful works that God has done in their life. Many people have become dependent upon miracles to simply sustain themselves in their faith and they never grow into a place of maturity where they become a miracle for someone else. The western church has become spoiled, traveling from one move of God to the next and from one church service to the next like a drug addict looking for their fix. I do encourage seeking and I still love having encounters, but how many do you really need before you begin to do the things that God has called you to do?

As discussed in previous chapters, the ancients believed that it was possible to be contacted by angelic forces in the same way that it was possible for demons to petition

Part 4
Beings of Light

people. There are several scriptures in the New Testament that speak about angelic etiquette if you will. Colossians 2:18 reads

LET NO MAN BEGUILE YOU OF YOUR REWARD IN A VOLUNTARY HUMILITY AND WORSHIPPING OF ANGELS, INTRUDING INTO THOSE THINGS WHICH HE HATH NOT SEEN, VAINLY PUFFED UP BY HIS FLESHLY MIND.

This is a warning about the worshipping of angels as some would like to do. Angels do not and should not receive worship, yet when mortals are in the presence of such majestic beings it oftentimes is the first thing that they want to do. There are instances where men would fall down on their faces in fear at the appearances of an angel in reverence or worship. In most cases the angel would tell them to get up and stop what they were doing because it was God alone who should receive praise. The scripture also says in Galatians 1:8

BUT THOUGH WE, OR AN ANGEL FROM HEAVEN, PREACH ANY OTHER GOSPEL UNTO YOU THAN THAT WHICH WE HAVE PREACHED UNTO YOU, LET HIM BE ACCURSED.

This also implies that angels communicate with humans, but it is also a warning not to depart from sound doctrine even if it was administered by an angel from heaven. This is a little strange coming from the one sharing his theology that was received from an angelic encounter with Jesus. On his journey to Damascus, Paul encountered a great light that blinded him. Paul immediately fell to his face and spoke with Jesus through the light. The men that accompanied Paul heard the voice but did not see the light. In shock Paul was led to Damascus where for three days he fasted and remained blind. This encounter changed the course of Paul's life forever. This enforces the notion that angelic encounters are not just for the thrill of it. In many circles so called angelic encounters are talked about like the weather, but these encounters leave no trace or evidence. How many angelic or demonic encounters does it take before you get the message? Is it seventeen? Is it four? What is the number? Biblically speaking when someone had an encounter with the other side they were forever changed. It had meaning and I believe they still do today. Everyone claims that they have had encounters with the divine and maybe they have, but what evidence do they have? People want proof. This generation desires a sign. There are sects of Christianity in the West that claim that heavy clouds of Gods glory appear during their services. Some claim that gold dust falls from heaven during their worship encounters, while still others receive angel feathers and precious stones such as diamonds and rubies that appear out of thin air. Is this proof that angels or the divine is among us? I am not sure. These manifestations can be easily faked and some have admitted in doing so to build the faith of those around them. I do still believe in contact and have touched the other side on many occasions, but why believe even me? What proof do I have? People make this stuff up every day and end up with books on the New York's Time's best sellers list. Some parents coax their children into telling stories of past lives or near death experiences so they can write books and get movie deals, only to later admit that they made it all up. Some people will do anything for fame or recognition.

This happened a few years ago on the news with the story of "Balloon Boy". Balloon Boy's dad built a hot air balloon in their backyard shaped like a UFO. While they were filming it, the balloon came untethered with the kid inside. The balloon took off flying hundreds of feet into the air and traveling through town being pushed by the wind. The dad immediately ran and called 911 and the local news. A huge rescue mission ensued and they were eventually able to bring the balloon safely back to the ground, only to realize

Part 4
Beings of Light

that Balloon Boy was nowhere to be found. They panicked worrying that the boy had fallen out somewhere during his flight, but they soon got a call that the boy was at home all along hiding in a box in the attic. After everything was said and done, Balloon Boy and his family received many offers for interviews on all of the largest networks. During one of the interviews, the press asked Balloon Boy why he decided to go and hide in the attic and give his parents a scare like that. After a few moments of silence his dad told him to answer the questions and the boy replied "Because you told me to". This was dad's grand plan to "make it big" all long. For years dad had been looking for his big break to generate more fame after his fifteen minutes of notoriety on the television show "Wife Swap". When the local authorities caught wind of what really happened, Balloon Boy's dad was jailed and required to pay for the rescue efforts, helicopter and all. This shows you the depths that some people will go to in order to achieve fame and notoriety. They will lie, make up stories and even get their small children to do the same.

What is the proof someone can show of angelic contact? Are people making it up, or did they really come into contact with something out of this world? Throughout history, people have reported encounters with angels. This is recorded throughout every Holy book in existence and major religions have even formed after these angelic encounters. Moses had ecstatic angelic encounters that led him to write the Torah. Muhammad was visited by the angel Jibril, who revealed to him the beginnings of what would later become the Quran. The Apostle Paul was visited by a bright light said to be Jesus that inspired him to write the majority of the New Testament. The Angel Moroni is the angel that Joseph Smith stated visited him on numerous occasions that inspired him to write the Book of Mormon. President George Washington also claimed that he encountered an angel that appeared to him that gave him the vision of America. A copy of the account is in the Library of Congress in Washington DC. *"With these words the vision vanished, and I started from my seat and felt that I had seen a vision wherein had been shown to me the birth, progress, and destiny of the United States"*.

These are but a few examples given throughout culture of records of angelic contacts that shaped the lives of individuals during their journeys. Within each of these texts are mentions of numerous encounters that inspired many more people to fulfill their God given callings. When talking about angelic realms and angelic contact, I feel I must also mention Ufology. Very similar stories are happening today with extraterrestrial and interdimensional beings that we would refer to as angels, which will be explained in more detail in the next chapter. Angels are sent to assist in our life's journey and can appear in many different scenarios.

Many people recall having angelic experiences during a near death encounter. Children have even reported seeing angels on many occasions. It is believed that the veil of the spirit realm is thinner for children because they are closer to God and their eyes have not become calloused. The apostle Paul even speaks about us entertaining angels unawares. The word angel simply means messenger and can vary in meaning due to circumstance or situation. Angels can also show up as ministering spirits to help us during hard times and encourage us on our journey. Many people claim to work with angels during hands on healing and reiki sessions. This form of healing is referred to as light work. It is without question that the Bible is full of angelic encounters of many different types from Genesis to Revelation. For me the proof is now and always has been a life laid down and transformed by these encounters. I love to hear stories like these, but I cannot judge if someone really has experienced these realms by their confession alone. Some people are really good storytellers and others

Part 4
Beings of Light

have really great imaginations. Jesus tells us to judge all things according to their fruit. I will not simply take your word for it. Let me see your lifestyle and integrity. Again, I do not believe in encounters for the sake of encounters. When someone was visited by any type of other worldly being in the Bible, be it angels, spirits or demons, their life drastically changed. That's the proof I'm looking for. That's all I need. If you had the encounter it was for a reason and your life will prove it through your character and ambition. This goes back to the first two scriptures I shared which act as a warning concerning angels.

Spirit Realm: Angels, Demons, Spirits and the Sovereignty of God

Migne's Patrologia Latina, vol 210, col. 267, 268

Part 4
Beings of Light

Novena

A Novena is a series of prayers that are recited for 9 days straight or 9 hours straight. The word itself is Latin for 9. A Novena is offered as a sacrifice to God because it is a sign of devotion. During this prayer devotion, the person saying the Novena speaks a specific request or intention. At the end of the 9 days or 9 hours, the person is said to receive the answer to their prayer. Novenas are practiced in the Catholic faith and are also used as invocations to summon angelic assistance. These prayers can be recited to call upon angels as well as Jesus, Mother Mary and the Saints of old. The prayers are often derived from devotional prayer books, or consist of the recitation of the rosary (a "rosary Novena"). They can also consist of short prayers through the day.

NOVENA TO ST. MICHAEL THE ARCHANGEL
(pray for 9 days or 9 hours straight)

Saint Michael the Archangel,
loyal champion of God and His People.
I turn to you with confidence
and seek your powerful intercession.
For the love of God,
Who made you so glorious in grace and power,
and for the love of the Mother of Jesus, the Queen of the Angels,
be pleased to hear our prayer.
You know the value of our souls in the eyes of God.
May no stain of evil ever disfigure its beauty.
Help us to conquer the evil spirit who tempts us.
We desire to imitate your loyalty to God and Holy Mother
and your great love for God and people.
And since you are God's messenger for the care of His people,
we entrust to you these special intentions:

Spirit Realm: Angels, Demons, Spirits and the Sovereignty of God

...specific intentions are stated here....
Lord, hear and grant our special intentions for this Novena.
Amen.

Working with angels and asking for angelic assistance is nothing new concerning faith. Although the verbiage may change, the spirit of the prayers is usually very similar. A Jewish nightly bedtime prayer asking for angelic protection reads as follows

"To God Almighty, the Lord of Israel: May Michael be at my right hand, Gabriel at my left hand, before me Raphael and behind me Uriel, and above me the divine presence of God."

Part 4
Beings of Light

Spirit Realm: Angels, Demons, Spirits and the Sovereignty of God

PART 5
ALIENS, ANGELS AND UFOS

Augsburger Wunderzeichenbuch, Folio 52 (Comet mit einem grosen Schwantz, 1401

I believe that the devout study of angels will eventually lead a person to the research of UFOs and Aliens. Throughout the Bible, we read about people encountering angels in various forms. In Daniel chapter 10, Daniel is visited by an angel during a fast and the angel tells him that he would have come sooner but he was delayed by The Prince of Persia. The Prince of Persia is what is known as a principality, power or a territorial spirit that is given authority over a region because of the deeds of the people. The angel then tells Daniel that he was assisted by the archangel Michael to help him overcome the principality. This portion of scripture shows that that angels travel from heaven to Earth relaying messages between God and men. I believe that what many are seeing in the sky and are calling UFOs are actually angels of the Lord, or the Hosts of heaven. The book of Enoch goes into much detail saying that even the stars are living and are communicate. They are said to record the deeds of mankind and report them back to God each night.

Chariots of Fire

The Hebrew word for Chariot is the word Merkaba, which literally translates to Vehicle. It was something that a person or being traveled in. These Chariots on many occasions are said to be carried or fueled by fire. The Israelites followed the presence of God as it communicated with them in the form of a cloud by day and fire by night. In many UFO sightings, people have reported to have seen what they call ships that look like clouds during the day and ships that seem to be made of fire during the night. In Ufology people are very familiar with cloud ships and plasma ships. The cloud ships are UFO craft that look like little clouds flying, because some of these smaller crafts hide inside of the clouds as to not be seen by humans. In the Old Testament, God spoke audibly with people communicating as a voice in the clouds. In the New Testament when Jesus is being baptized by John, a voice speaks from the clouds saying "Behold, this is my beloved son; hear him". The Bible also states that God "rides upon the clouds" and in Acts 1:9 Jesus actually ascends into heaven into a cloud.

In ufology there is also what is known as light or plasma ships. The connection can be made back to the chariots or vehicles of fire in the Bible. Some have stated that they are ships that are carrying occupants and others say that these so called ships are actually living entities like the Seraphim, because some of them change shape and seem to be alive. The Seraphim are a sect of angels believed to surround the throne of God. When mentioned in Isaiah 6, they had six wings. With two they covered their faces, with two they covered their feet, and with two they flew. They

Spirit Realm: Angels, Demons, Spirits and the Sovereignty of God

continually sing praises unto the creator shouting "Holy, holy, holy is the Lord of hosts; the whole earth is full of his glory." It is interesting to note that word Seraphim literally translates to "fiery serpents". These angels are made out of the fire of God and are said to carry the knowledge of the higher realms of heaven. The word serpent here is interesting for two reasons. The first is that some people have reported seeing beings in the sky that actually looked like large snakes. Secondly, in antiquity serpents were synonymous with knowledge referring to the Seraphim carrying the sacred knowledge of God.

"The Crucifixion" 1350 Visoki Decani Monestary in Kosovo, Serbia

Part 5
Aliens, Angels and UFOs

The CE5 Contact Initiative Summoning Angels / UFOs

There are countless books available on the topic of contacting or summoning angels and communicating with beings on the other side. One particular topic of interest is what is known as the CE5 Initiative meaning Close Encounters of The Fifth Kind. This is not explained as a UFO contacting you, but where you contact them. This can be done in a variety of ways. The most common way this is done is while stargazing. The person usually gets themselves in a comfortable state ready to initiate contact. Intention is key because expectation usually brings about manifestation. The person then may begin praying inwardly or outwardly, either communicating with God or trying to make contact with the beings above. During this process the person may begin to see strange aerial phenomena or what appears to be stars moving then stopping or immediately changing direction. People have also reported that these lights will also being to blink almost as if they are trying to communicate by using a type of Morse code. After a connection like this happens, the person may begin to receive telepathic messages in the form of inward impressions or ideas sent from the ship / beings. This practice can be done alone or in group settings. I have had personal experiences in both and have seen things that have changed my life in amazing ways. These experiences impart the notion that the other side is real. People may debate about what actually is going on and try to explain these sightings away but for me it reiterates the fact that God, Heaven and the Spirit Realm are real. It shows that Heaven is not just some other realm that we cross over to when we die but that it is a place that physically exists out there beyond the stars. As we are gazing into the night sky we are literally gazing into eternity. The Bible and many other sacred texts tell of stories of angels that travel from Heaven to Earth as a place that literally exists. For me it builds my faith and tends to bring about some validity to the stories.

Ego Quid Videret by Drew Meger

I was always infatuated with aliens as a child but it was mostly through fear based horror movies that I watched. I was terribly afraid of aliens because I felt that they were the monsters that most likely exist. I remember watching the movie "A Fire In The Sky" that was supposedly based on the true story of Travis Walton's abduction experience. This movie scared me as a child because of the demonic humanoid looking aliens in the movie that could kidnap a person at will and keep them forever. This was a constant fear of mine. I remember even my backwoods Baptist pastor talking about this movie at church when I was

Part 5
Aliens, Angels and UFOs

around 7 years old. When I grew up I felt led to research the alien subject a little closer. I was led down more of the Christian understanding in the beginning, which still was the fear based teachings that aliens were demons. Almost entirely across the board all of the conservative views and Christian experts in the field of Ufology unanimously held to the view that aliens and UFOs were demonic fallen angels. The more I dug into this I couldn't help but hear them mention some of the names of the secular Ufologists, so I ended up looking into their work as well. I honestly really liked what I heard from them because I felt that the majority of them were approaching the subject from a non-biased standpoint. I felt as if they were looking at all of the information as a whole and coming up with other theories that made more sense than the blanket statement "They are all demonic". As I dug deeper into this research, I found a website entitled BibleUFO.com, which was the life work of Patrick Cooke. Patrick approached Ufology from a Christian and Biblical perspective but he didn't call everything demonic. Patrick was open to the fact that these beings and ships traveling from Heaven to Earth could be angelic in nature. BibleUFO.com was a massive website that basically took every angelic encounter in the Bible and explained how it lined up with Ufology. The website also tracked hundreds of historical evidence about UFO sightings dating back as early as 45,000 BC. As I picked apart this website, I listened to hours upon hours of interviews from Patrick Cooke and others who were more open to having this conversation. I also ended up finding this video on YouTube in 2011 of a man named Prophet Yahweh who claimed he could summon UFOs on demand and he actually did so for ABC News. This video blew me away and I got chills while watching it. Prophet Yahweh said that he could summon UFOs by using the ancient Hebrew Bible. The news crew followed him out to an open field. He then closed his eyes and began to pray while his hands stretched up towards heaven as he asked Yahweh for a sighting. Then suddenly this shiny white orb appeared and the ABC News broadcaster's mind was blown. They then called the local airport to see if there was anything reported to be in the air at that time and their answer was no. This video went viral and I ended up doing more research and watching many more videos of Prophet Yahweh summoning UFOs. When I studied under the Hebrew Israelites in the past, they mentioned the Chariots in the Bible. They spoke of how this was synonymous to UFOs because the Hebrew word for chariot simply means vehicle. With all this research and knowledge at hand, I wanted to have sightings myself and see if this "Summoning UFO" thing actually worked. I ended up going out early on the mornings that I worked (from 3:30 – 5am) to try and have my own sightings. Just like Prophet Yahweh, I would lift my hands to Heaven and ask God for a sighting. "If these are your heavenly angels, Elohim, Seraphim or Cherubim please allow me to see one, please allow one to pass me by". And then suddenly while in prayer, I began to see lights appear in the sky next to stars and start moving. These lights would do really weird aerial phenomena like making 90 degree turns and stop on a dime and almost pretend to be stars in the night sky. These sightings blew my mind and I couldn't wait to get to work every day so that I could go out and try and make contact again. I became obsessed with having these encounters and have seen things in the heavens that challenged my theology and have changed my life forever.

By The Stars of Orion

While driving for my old delivery company, I stopped at an exit right past Pensacola Florida to spend a few minutes stargazing and to enjoy the view and the cool breeze. I got out and began to name off all of the constellations and stars that I knew. I then began to pray and sing this new song that I wrote to God that is really powerful. I was

Part 5
Aliens, Angels and UFOs

looking up at the constellation Orion and then I turned away. When I looked back at the belt of Orion I saw that it was lit very brightly and it caught my attention because it was too bright! I then looked a little higher and saw that it was not Orion's belt that I was seeing at all, but what looked to be three bright stars in the position of the belt. The stars were aligned like Orion's belt, but were actually a bit below the constellation. As soon as I realized this, the two stars on each end began to move towards the constellation. The lights on each end began to move up and one started to zig zag a little towards the other. They moved towards the constellation Orion and lost their brightness as the appeared to go into the constellation. The other star remained in the place. I ran back to my work truck to get my camera to see if I could get any video, but my camera could not pick up any light in the sky because it was a low quality camera phone. The middle light I saw was actually the star Rigel lower down in the constellation Orion.

The founder of the Seventh Day Adventist church Ellen G. White would often have visions from heaven and fall into trances during worship. One of her visions was of the constellation Orion. She said, "Dark heavy clouds came up and clashed against each other. The atmosphere parted and rolled back; then we could look up through the open space in Orion, whence came the voice of God. The Holy City will come down through that open space." This is the gateway from our part of the universe into the central Heaven where God dwells. Here we see Ellen making the following conjectures.

1. There is an opening or stargate into "a region more enlightened"

2. Orion is a gateway between our universe and the dwelling place of God

3. The voice of God comes through an "open space in Orion"

4. The "holy city" will come to earth through the opening in Orion

There is a mystery associated with the Orion Constellation found in indigenous cultures all over the world that dates back to ancient Egypt. Ancient alchemists speak about man's connection to the Orion Nebula and its relation to the human body and consciousness. The Orion Nebula has been depicted by some of the greatest masters in religious art including Michelangelo, El Greco, Bernini, and others, yet the intimate knowledge of the Orion Nebula found mysteriously in these paintings precedes the discovery of the telescope and still would require technology that rivals some of our most powerful telescopes today.

Over My House

I have been in deep levels of prayer and meditation and have felt the angelic presence around me. I have felt them scanning my body from the top of my head to the bottoms of my feet before initiating contact or leading me on a journey within. The first time this happened fear gripped me and the feeling was so surreal that I opened my eyes to see if the being was really there. With my eyes closed, I could clearly see the silhouette of a humanoid being resembling an alien grey but its entire body was filled with green light. Those of the spiritual paths in Egypt believe this to be an initiation into the order of Melchezidek where Melchezidek himself must appear to you by appearing in green light. I remember a story that James Gilliland shared about meditating in his home while telepathically communicating with angelic beings. When his sister arrived

Part 5
Aliens, Angels and UFOs

to the house, she ran inside hysterically saying that there was a UFO hovering over their house while James was having this encounter.

One particular night I was walking outside with my daughter asking the father to show us some chariots. I wasn't seeing much in my backyard so we walked to the front. I then looked up after asking the father to open up my eyes to see a chariot or a seraphim, as soon as I did I saw a streak of light with the most beautiful color tail following. I then thanked the Lord for this sighting and asked for another. As soon as I turned around to face the house I saw a huge chariot descending just above the treetops and coming towards us.

I was in a state of total shock, I yelled to my daughter, "Go inside and hurry!" Then I told her, "Wait come back...no no no, go inside!" She said, "What do you want me to do? Go in or stay out?" I said, "Go in and get momma." As soon as I started to panic, the craft suddenly took a left turn. It was going fairly slow and never made a sound. The feeling was so surreal. I didn't think I would see one this close, most of the ones I've seen up to this point were far up. All I could really see was kind of a silhouette with 3 bright lights, almost like headlights. When asked if it came close enough for me to throw a rock and hit it, I said, "No not me but maybe Peyton Manning could."

If I were to write down all of my experiences with what we call UFOs it would surely take up the majority of this book. However, this book is just to give you an overview about how these entities work in the spirit realm and interact with humanity. I have seen cigar shaped UFOs in broad daylight, had telepathic communication with the heavenly hosts in the night sky and on one occasion had a fleet of over seventy ships appear in broad daylight that allowed me to see them before cloaking.

The Divine In Art

There is a sense of awe and wonder when talking about encounters with the other side. When we catch a glimpse of eternity, it tends to help us feel that we are eternal and the trivial minute problems of the day seem to get a lot smaller. Whether it is through stargazing or having ecstatic religious experiences, something of beauty is imparted to the individual that tends to come out through creativity and art. For me, it is embodied within my music and podcast and it acts as a portal where the listener is taken on a journey to the very place where I encountered the divine. It stirs something ancient and majestic up within us, imparting awe and wonder to the beholder. These experiences can be articulated through any medium imaginable such as books, paintings music etc. To some, it would seem like form of escapism or a way to run from ones problems into the fantasy world. I've found that the feeling you receive when you find out that fantasy is not that far off from reality is incredible. Throughout history, our ancestors left cave art with sketches of alien-like beings and gods covering the walls. The renaissance brings about even more questions when it comes to the art. There are many religious paintings that show Jesus hanging on the cross with little men driving space craft in the background dating back to the 1400's. Other depictions show Mother Mary with baby Jesus, and in the background there is a man looking at a UFO.

Part 5
Aliens, Angels and UFOs

The Madonna with Saint Giovannino Attributed to Arcangelo di Jacopo del Sellaio

Art has a way of making the imagination manifest to the world and embodying an experience by trapping it in time. Art was also used as a means of propaganda by swaying the opinion of the masses, such as in Nazi Germany. Posters, cartoons and comics all had political themes that were used to convince the population to normalize things that they wouldn't usually accept. The Jews were depicted as disgusting terrifying monsters, and the general population accepted it as truth. This led to Jews being attacked in the streets and ultimately caused the genocide of an entire population of innocent people. Repetition reduces resistance and the more and more we hear or see an idea we tend to let our guard down and become desensitized and allow things we wouldn't normally accept. This deep concept is also used in marketing campaigns, logos and branding all the way from the colors, shape and jingles that are used by big corporations to sell us things. This is known as color psychology.

Spirit Realm: Angels, Demons, Spirits and the Sovereignty of God

Part 5
Aliens, Angels and UFOs

Part 6
Plant Medicine

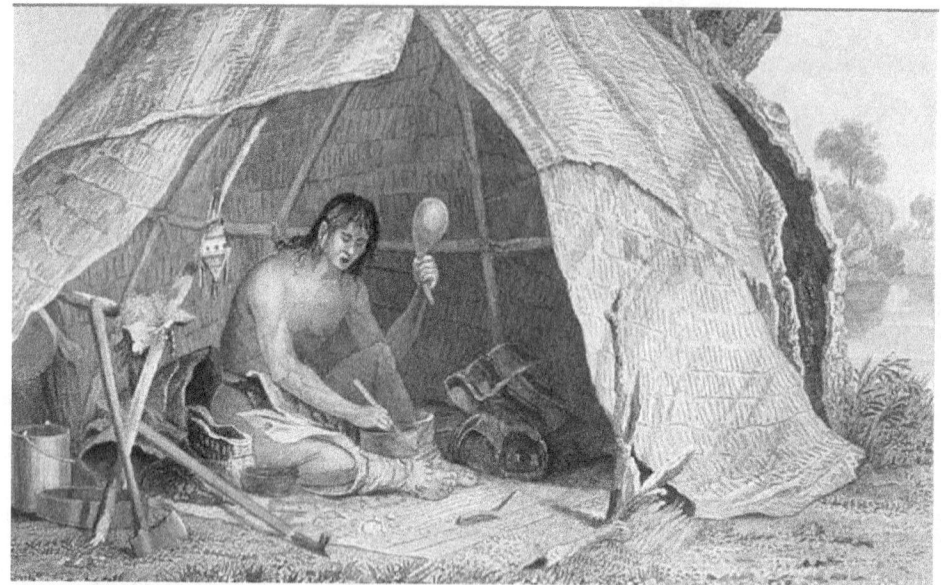

Indian Medicine Man from an 1875 Eastman engraving. National Library of Medicine.

In recent times there has been resurgence in the popularity of the idea of sacred plant medicine or psychedelics. It is becoming more mainstream as westerners are seeking to find enlightenment and have no choice but to look to the East. I am sure that it has something to do with the internet. We are privy to new information daily. People are becoming more open about their experiences with plant medicines and that allows others to consider it as well. The Joe Rogan Podcast has been a huge tool in getting this information out to people who would probably never try such a thing. Joe has been very open about his own personal experiences and has had many guests on his podcast who talk about the impact that plant medicine has had on their lives. As someone who has spent time in and out of the other realms and has

Part 6
Plant Medicine

personally dealt with demonic possession, the idea of psychedelics scared the hell out of me. I did not want to turn my consciousness over to an entity and have no say-so for any length of time, even if only for a few hours. Dealing with the demonic, you have to be on guard to keep the demons of the past from coming back. It is not smart to open a door that God has already shut behind you, for fear of the evil spirits returning with several greater than themselves. This is the fear many Christians have today when it comes to psychedelics and plant medicine and the reason I have caught so much backlash for speaking on the subject. But I understand, this should be a concern for people and was most definitely a concern for me also. I pride myself on the fact that I am able to achieve heightened states of consciousness through meditation, halotropic breath work and kundalini yoga and I didn't need any type of "substance" to do so. Yet the more and more I listened to The Joe Rogan Podcast and his guests, the more interested I became with the subject. Joe has had guests on such as Aubrey Marcus and Amber Lyon, who both have amazing life changing stories about plant medicines such as psilocybin mushrooms and ayahuasca (DMT). Aubrey speaks about radical encounters that he has had with the medicine that has helped him deal with childhood trauma and has assisted him in dealing with his ego and overcoming his own personal demons. Amber speaks about coming to the end of her rope as an investigative journalist for CNN. She was dealing with immense depression and on a whim boarded a flight to the Amazon Rainforest to visit a shaman at an ayahuasca retreat center. She tells about going through the ceremony and finding healing. One of the things she mentioned was that throughout her years as a journalist she has interviewed some very dark individuals who have done very disgusting things. In her interview on The Joe Rogan Podcast Amber said that it felt like a piece of everyone's energy that she interviewed had rubbed off on her and that this had something to do with the way she was feeling. Both Aubrey and Amber in their stories of their ayahuasca ceremony speak about their healing and inward journey being assisted by different beings. They both spoke of The Elves. Amber said that she saw this long roll of film extend that represented her entire life and she would zoom in on different parts. While she was doing this, she said that she saw tiny elves doing work on her almost as if they were repairing her DNA. Aubrey speaks of similar encounters. Joe Rogan has had similar experiences with the elves and actually jokingly said that they looked like "Complex Sacred Geometric Patterns that are made of love and understanding". The psychonaut Terrence McKenna and his work has been a huge influence on Joe Rogan and Joe seems to try and mention him on his podcast every chance that he gets. McKenna also spoke about what he called the machine or fractal elves and believes that this is where our lore comes from about elves, fairies and gnomes. Most of the people who have had these life changing experiences while under the influence of plant medicine speak about encountering beings that are there to assist them. They also speak about the feeling of immense love and acceptance as they are oftentimes led through a life review by these conscious beings that are doing the work of God. McKenna spoke about the plant medicines such as psilocybin magic mushrooms possibly being some sort of "walkie talkie" or communication device put here by some higher intelligence of gods, aliens or angels that allows us the privilege to communicate with enlightened beings. One thing that McKenna has been quoted saying on the subject of UFOs and aliens is, "This is something I'm going to try and convince the UFO community of; what we drug people have that you don't is repeatability". Meaning that any time they wanted to communicate and interact with these beings all they had to do was ingest a magic mushroom and they were suddenly transported into these realms. Maybe this is the connection when it comes to trying to summon UFOs like Prophet

Part 6
Plant Medicine

Yahweh or myself. The benefit of being able to harness the repeatability is to be able to offer others a similar experience. McKenna also talked about the notion of magic mushrooms being a memory bank that holds all of the memories of galactic history and by ingesting them you are accessing this information. This information is commonly known as The Akashic Records. Some circles even believe that magic mushrooms were the forbidden fruit of the Bible, because if you partake of the fruit you are becoming like God knowing both good and evil.

After listening to hours and hours of podcasts, lectures and teachings on the subject I felt as if the mushrooms were calling out to me. I still approached the subject with some fear, but I was ready to have my experience.

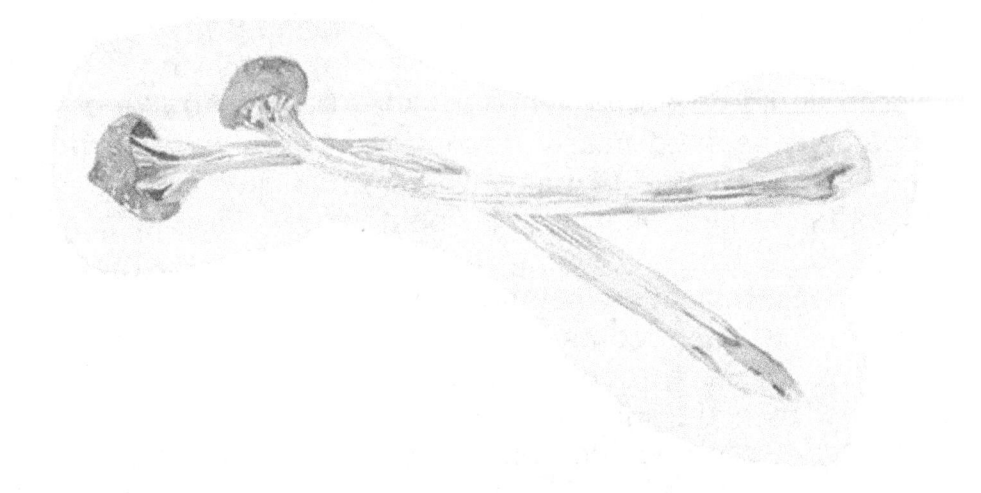

I got in touch with a close friend of mine Drew Gower who had already had a great many experiences with psilocybin mushrooms. We ended up booking a trip to New Orleans to try ingesting the mushrooms in a sensory deprivation tank. When we got to New Orleans, our first stop was a holistic healing center where we booked a guided meditation and reiki session. This felt like the perfect way to start our experience. After killing some time visiting Bourbon Street and checking out some great art, we headed to the float tank center. I was friends with the owner so he offered to let us to spend the night at the center. We took the sacrament and entered our separate float tanks. I ingested about 2 grams.

It was a beautiful first encounter for me, and the mushrooms were very introspective showing me things about my life and my journey thus far. I cut my float tank session a bit short because I had a bunch of information downloads coming to me that I felt that I needed to write down. I had this overwhelming feeling that I wanted to be a healer. I wanted to do something for a living that brought forth healing to people as an occupation. Maybe it was something that rubbed off on me after our visit with the reiki practitioner, because the thought of waking up every day and working with people to help them find healing almost instantly began to plague my mind. It seemed like something that was so far away and seemed like it would be out of reach for me. It seemed like a pipe dream. It seemed nearly impossible. There were all these reasons that came to mind why I could never do it. "I'm not that well-spoken so I could never lead a guided meditation" was something that seemed like a wall but still there was this overwhelming feeling of wanting to be a healer. The mushrooms seem to have a way to letting you view your life through the lens of God. It's as if you connect with the infinite power of the universe when you take them and you see your life objectively in third person yet through the eyes of love. As I began to have an inward dialogue with God about wanting to be a healer it was as if God spoke to me and said, "You already are. You are not 'going to be one'; your whole life is based around helping people find healing already. If it is something outside of yourself you will never find it. All of this already exists within you." This life review got even deeper and the voice began to show me even more things in my life that are based around healing, including my music. So something at first that seemed so far and so unattainable now came into better focus. It showed me that I am already on the journey. It was not something that I needed to become, but is something that I AM. I then began to receive instructions on how to bring this into fruition. Practical steps that I needed to manifest my destiny. I wrote all of this down. I was also shown some character flaws and things that I needed to let go of in order to get to the next level in my journey. I wrote those down too and I was excited to take the next steps. When asked about hallucinating or seeing strange things during the mushroom experience, my response is that I only had closed eye visuals and saw complex sacred geometry, gears and symbols with my eyes closed, but nothing with my eyes open. It was definitely a philosophical experience and life review encounter.

My friend Drew had a similar experience as well, which he goes into greater detail about in his book "Living Life with No Days Off". I was blessed to be asked to write the foreword for his book. After our journey, we returned home and I was excited to unpack all of the information that I had received during the trip and I knew that it would take the next few months to do so. I ended up doing several podcasts as a guest on other people's shows and talking about my experience and writing about some of it in my music. I started speaking on the subject almost as if I were an expert after my only time using psilocybin. I soon got checked for doing this.

Manifestation

A few weeks later a book came across my path entitled *The Alchemist* by Paulo Coelho and this book radically sparked something within my heart to pursue my dreams.

In short, the book is about a boy who leaves home set out on a journey to find this hidden treasure. On his journey, he runs into characters that make him think about his life choices and journey. Essentially the book is an allegory about our own journey, pursuing our destiny and recapturing the dreams that we had when we were children. The book is not about some young man on his journey, it's about US on OUR journey. Having my psilocybin experience coupled with reading this book seemed to light a huge fire within me. It ignited an urgency to set out and start trying to bring the vision that I received into fruition. I was very excited but this was still something very scary to me, yet having these two experiences really changed me. The book reminds you to recapture the dream you had as a child, but all the while it forced me to see that so many people are stuck in their own day to day lives simply by default. The majority of people that I encountered on a daily basis had given up on their dreams and just settled. This broke my heart, and still does. I looked at my boss who had been with the company for over 20 years and I saw how angry and bitter he had become over time. I thought to myself, 'I'm sure this was not his dream as a child; to work at a company where he is expendable and not happy.' Somewhere along the way he gave up on his dream. Inward reflection made me look at my life at the age of 33 and know that somewhere along the line I gave up on my dream. If I looked hard enough I could tell when the exact time was.

So, was I destined to just be a truck driver for the rest of my life? Did the dream really pass me by? I know what I felt inside and the things that God had shown me, but my situation looked like the total opposite. This would drive me to tears thinking about it. What age should you give up on your dream? What age do you buckle down and just accept things the way they are and forget about what could be just a pipe dream or vain imaginations? The answer is NEVER. You must fight for what you believe in.

Part 6
Plant Medicine

Nothing comes overnight and anything worth doing is worth doing right. I arrived at this strange place mentally where I could clearly see where I was supposed to be and it was liberating, because I felt like God was the one showing me. On the other hand, there was depression setting in because it seemed so far out of reach. I believe that plant medicine can work to assist us on our journey to get a vision for ourselves about how to get to where we want to be. If we listen closely enough they will communicate a few steps about how to get started also. The medicines have the ability to create new perspective, heal depression and addictions, and I also believe that in some cases they can cause depression. When you go on a psychedelic journey and see behind the veil, you come face to face with eternity. You end up in a place where there is no time or space, in a place beaming with life. You receive universal truths about reality, love and the power of the now moment. You may interact with heavenly beings or earth and nature spirits and have these amazing truths communicated to you about your destiny and how to manifest it. But when you return back to your job at the warehouse, back to the construction job site or wherever it is that you just seemed to land by default, if you do not put those principals you learned into practice it will plague you. It will birth an even greater depression within you because you have seen what is possible. That's what it did for me, so I began to step out in faith. I began to study divine healing, reiki, and guided meditation, coupled with my own spiritual beliefs that I already practiced daily and I put myself out there. During one of my interviews on someone else's show, they announced that I was offering private intuitive healing sessions and after the show I had my first two bookings. These sessions blew my mind because as I began to council my clients and lead them into deep meditation, they were able to find spiritual freedom. This is something that I've been practicing for years in person but in my mind there was a disconnect because these people I was working with via video chat were in other parts of the world. As I led them into the trance state and began to send healing energies to them, they would feel a strong presence of peace come over them and they would begin to weep. Some of them would completely stop smoking and quit other addictions, while others found healing and forgiveness for childhood traumas. Each situation was different, but I was able to facilitate an encounter for them that left a mark on their life. Within two weeks I was booked up with private sessions with people from all over the world and this happened so quickly that was stunned. I'm not sure if I was ready for it to happen so fast because in my mind it would take years for me to get good at it and I would need to get better at speaking etc. I had all these fears and still could count so many reasons why I shouldn't do this, but the joy that it brought me to be one step closer to my destiny was so overwhelming. I had manifested this. I created it.

Part 6
Plant Medicine

The Golden Teachers

Throughout my journey, my friend Drew encouraged me along the way. I can't emphasize how important and necessary it is to have people in your corner who are on the journey with you. Not 'yes-men', which are people who just go along with whatever you say, but people who truly believe in you and want the best for you. There is not a price that you can put on that kind of genuine friendship. A few months later, I told Drew that I was working on a song about my psilocybin experience. I told him that I wanted to name the song *Golden Teachers* after a strain of stronger psilocybin mushrooms that Drew had told me about. Drew replied, "But you've never had the Golden Teachers." I said, "I know, but I really like the name." Drew then said that maybe we should plan another trip where I could experience them, so I agreed. I was a little more afraid this time because the Golden Teacher strain of mushrooms were a great deal stronger, but at this point I'm an expert right? I contacted a few Christian brothers who I knew were open and curious about mushroom experiences after doing their own research and hearing me talk about how life changing the experience was and we set a date. We booked a cabin in the woods and we called it a men's getaway.

I continued to strongly emphasize with everyone that this should be a time of reflection and direction and shouldn't be taken lightly. Some of us fasted a few days that week while others cut meat out of their diets to prepare before the getaway. Each of us had some things that we wanted to bring before God and saw this as a perfect opportunity to do so. One of the other guys was dealing with an opiate addiction that he wanted to kick. Another had marriage problems. Another was dealing with obesity. The rest of us just wanted to ask for a little more direction in life. There was a total of six of us who showed up to the event. We had a great time of fellowship, playing football and walking the trails out in nature all while knowing that we were just really killing time before consuming the sacrament. As the sun began to go down, we made our way back to the cabin where I led everyone in prayer. We played a few songs on the guitar together and then got into some chanting. Drew then handed out everyone's portions of the sacrament. In my first experience I did 2 grams of the Hawaiians, but this time I was going to go ahead and do a hero dose of the much stronger strain of Golden Teachers. I partook of at least 5 grams. We all then sat back and wait for them to kick in just talking and laughing to try and rid ourselves of the nervousness of what was to come. Only three of the

Part 6
Plant Medicine

six of us had used the mushrooms before and although this was my second time, I thought I was already an expert. As the sacrament began to kick in I started to feel a little weird. I got up off of the couch and went outside to get some fresh air and looked up at the trees. As I did this, I saw a strange green webbing that seemed to be the fabric that held everything together. I experienced this with my eyes open. I began to feel a bit woozier and immediately fear gripped me. What if I took too much? I definitely took way more than last time and these are stronger! What if these were the wrong kind? What if they are the poisonous kind? What if I die? Can I make this stop? If I called the police department can they help me? No, I knew I'd still have to ride this out. All of these fears overtook me. I had done mushrooms before but they didn't feel like this. This feels like what they describe on some DMT Ayahuasca trips, not mushrooms. I then leaned over the porch railing and proceed to throw up. 'Maybe this will get some of it out of my system,' I thought. After that I walked inside and sat down on the couch with the rest of the guys and looked at Drew. I told Drew, "I'm not feeling so well bro. I feel like it's trying to pull me." He said, "It's supposed to, stop fighting it and let it take you." Fighting it was exactly what I was doing. I was trying my best to hang on and the Golden Teachers were trying to take me somewhere else. I said ok, quit fighting and lay back on the couch. As I closed my eyes, I heard a voice and felt overshadowed by the presence of two beings. One of them spoke to me and said "Is this TruthSeekah? Is this the one who has been doing interviews acting as if he is an expert on plant medicines? Is this the one who is releasing music and writing lyrics about the secrets of heaven, astral travel and star gates like it's no big deal?" The other said "Yes, this is he." They communicated with me and let me know that what I was doing with the subject matter of my music is a very big deal and not to be taken lightly, and that sharing the secrets of the universe comes with a high price. "Are you sure that you are willing to keep going? Do you really want to do this?" they said. I thought about what they said for a minute and then said, "Yes." They said, "Ok, you are TruthSeekah right?" I said yes, then they replied, "Ok, we're just trying to make sure we have the right one. We have something to show you." and immediately I felt like I was sucked out of my body through a portal and I was traveling down a wormhole. Everything was moving so fast but as I let go, the fear left as well. I was in another realm, a world within a world. Colors, lights, and sounds galore filled this other realm that I was transported to and it was all so beautiful. The colors were alive, you could feel them, and everything worked together in perfect unison. This was a place of universal love and bliss. In this realm I felt connected to the entire universe and all sentient beings. There was an overwhelming sense of oneness. Here everything is OK. There is no stress, no bills, and no personas, only divine love. The angelic teachers then told me that this is the place that humans will return to when we pass. The cabin that we were in was on Indian land and I am part Poarch Creek Indian. They told me that many of my ancestors have been here as well and this was a part of my initiation. After a few minutes passed, which seemed like an eternity to me, I opened my eyes. We all looked around at one another in awe and amazement. I looked at Drew and he was smiling. We all then tried to articulate what we were seeing on the other side but it sounded crazy trying to express in words the colors, complex geometry and communications we received in the other realms. Then, almost like a countdown I felt it coming back and told the guys to get ready because it was coming back again. It almost felt like we were on a roller coaster ride together climbing up to the peak getting ready to plunge down again into the depths of this other world. I said, "Here it comes!" and like clockwork we reached the peak. Click, Click, Click, Click….. ZOOM! Again all of us together were sucked into another portal and down the rollercoaster experiencing the beauty and splendor of this other realm. After a few minutes we all opened our eyes together and once again tried to explain what we were seeing and feeling. We had some soft beautiful worship music on in the background and as we begin to just worship God and thank Him for this experience, we could feel His presence in the room. Tears began to flow down our faces as we sat in the majesty of God. The truths that were experienced through the worship music had so much more meaning in this state. We could also feel the intention behind the music, so as the music played we could feel the heart of the musician with every strum of the guitar and snare of the drum. We were totally undone and overwhelmed by the love and presence of God. It's one thing to know deep down that you are loved by God but it's a totally different sensation when you can tangibly feel that love all over your body and radiating down deep into your core cleansing you while the music is being played over you. You don't have to be under the influence of plant teachers to encounter this. I have experienced similar states of ecstatic bliss many times before in deep worship. The fruit that an experience like this produces in the heart of an individual is immeasurable.

Spirit Realm: Angels, Demons, Spirits and the Sovereignty of God

Part 7
Entering The Trance State

Jeremiah's Vision of the Seething Pot. Scripture Illustrated 1806

The Bible and The Trance State

Did you know that the biblical disciples and prophets regularly practiced trance states? The scripture says he who dwells in the secret place of the most high shall abide in the shadow of the Almighty. This is symbolic in the Old Testament as we see David running from his enemies and in hiding in the cave. Our enemies symbolize our cares and worries of this world and the shadow of the Almighty is the secret place of prayer we enter into with God through hypnotic trance. This trance state of meditation is also known as the secret place. Many

Part 7
Entering The Trance State

times, the Jewish people would pull their prayer shawl over their heads and cover their faces to go into the prayer closet to commune with God. Jesus often would go on top of mountains or within them for prolonged periods of time to pray and seek God. This is very similar of what we see yogis and gurus doing in the East by going on top of and deep into mountains to fast and meditate. The trance state is the place that we enter into through meditation. This is the place of mindfulness where we are able to experience the now moment. This is also the place that we go to commune with God one on one.

The Bible is full of mysticism and spiritual encounters and it would be absurd overlook this sacred text. The Bible is filled with deep allegory and advanced spirituality. Jesus and his disciples were some of the most spiritual people to walk the face of the planet. They had a strict discipline that catered to their spiritual walk. Some of their daily spiritual encounters included fasting, dream symbolism, communicating with angels, being raptured out of body to heaven, hearing the voice of God, divination, removing unclean spirits from people, demonstrating supernatural healings, bi-location, going in and out of trances and even more. The Church of the West largely assumes that these were one-time experiences that Jesus, the prophets and the disciples experienced, but we must understand that Christianity started out as a spiritual practice in the East before it became a religion in the West. One must note that biblical Christianity looks nothing like western church or Catholicism. These were men given to devotion and had daily encounters with the supernatural.

During worship services at most churches, people are entering into hypnotic trances and don't even know it. Just imagine, people standing still with their hands in the air worshiping God with their eyes closed from anywhere of 30 to 45 minutes while music is being played. They are usually chanting and using mantras by repeating a part of the song over and over like "I Love you, I love You, I Love You" etc. Doing this while music is being played is one of the fastest ways to enter into hypnotic trance. In this hypnotic trance like state, people often report feeling the presence of God, seeing angels, overcoming addictions and having their burdens lifted, so I would never denounce or demonize these practices. Rather, I applaud them and I'll give you more Biblical examples for this practice. Here are a few scriptures that talk about encounters with the trance state.

AND NOW WHY TARRIEST THOU? ARISE, AND BE BAPTIZED, AND WASH AWAY THY SINS, CALLING ON THE NAME OF THE LORD. AND IT CAME TO PASS, THAT, WHEN I WAS COME AGAIN TO JERUSALEM, EVEN WHILE I PRAYED IN THE TEMPLE, I WAS IN A TRANCE; AND SAW HIM SAYING UNTO ME, MAKE HASTE, AND GET THEE QUICKLY OUT OF JERUSALEM: FOR THEY WILL NOT RECEIVE THY TESTIMONY CONCERNING ME. – ACTS 22:16-18

Here we find Paul going into a deep trance during a large prayer gathering within the temple. This practice still occurs today with Christians in a large church setting, small group or even in their personal devotional prayer time alone. We also see The Apostle Peter in Acts 11:4 ,

BUT PETER REHEARSED THE MATTER FROM THE BEGINNING, AND EXPOUNDED IT BY ORDER UNTO THEM, SAYING, I WAS IN THE CITY OF JOPPA PRAYING: AND IN A TRANCE I SAW A VISION, A CERTAIN VESSEL DESCEND, AS IT HAD BEEN A GREAT SHEET, LET DOWN FROM HEAVEN BY FOUR CORNERS; AND IT CAME EVEN TO ME.

Part 7
Entering The Trance State

Treasures of the Bible by Henry Davenport Northrop, 1894

In this particular instance, Peter saw a vision during a trance where God showed him what to do at a future time. It was actually shown to him through dream symbolism that he would have to interpret in order to get the meaning.

Also in Numbers 24:16
HE HATH SAID, WHICH HEARD THE WORDS OF GOD, AND KNEW THE KNOWLEDGE OF THE MOST HIGH, WHICH SAW THE VISION OF THE ALMIGHTY, FALLING INTO A TRANCE, BUT HAVING HIS EYES OPEN

These are just a few scriptures that show the prophets and disciples going in and out of trances. All of the practices mentioned help the believer to walk in the spirit and should accompany our daily spiritual life.

Spirit Realm: Angels, Demons, Spirits and the Sovereignty of God

Opening The Third Eye

Fig. 187. The Psycho-Magnetic Curves.

Illustration from Edwin D. Babbitt's The Principles of Light and Color (1878) — Source.

With the influx of spiritual articles on the internet, we see people showing you chants and mantras on how to "open your third eye." However, everyone is born with their third eye or Pineal Gland already opened. This is the reason why children and infants are sensitive to seeing spirits and the ghosts of deceased relatives. When you are born you are as close to the spirit realm as you will ever be, but due to societal conditioning and the intake of chemicals through processed foods, our third eye begins to become calcified. The third eye is how we are able to see into the spirit realm and peer beyond the veil of reality as we know it. The third eye isn't closed or in a state of having never been opened. We have simply forgotten how to use it. There are practices that help us to stimulate our third eye and remember how to see through it again. The practices below will help guide you into the trance state, which makes us more sensitive to other dimensions by stimulating our extra sensory perception. These techniques and daily practices can be done to help strengthen your third eye for better spiritual vision and clarity. The third eye acts as a muscle. It must be trained and conditioned to get stronger. Many ancient orders would take notice of their children who were more prone to sensing spiritual dimensions and they catered to it. They had education in place to teach them to better use these natural abilities. We must also educate ourselves with similar practices that were commonly known by our ancestors. Here are just a few techniques that will help you stimulate your third eye and become more in tune with the trance state.

Chanting

Chanting the OHM (AUM) mantra and other lower sounding tones is very powerful in physically vibrating the pineal gland to stimulate its function. This tone will cleanse your aura and naturally produces feelings of oneness with the universe. Chanting techniques also give us access to the power of the spoken word. Repetitively chanting positive affirmations or sacred mantras over ourselves has great power. Positive affirmations have been known to rid people of addictions and create healthier ways of thinking. Chanting in a relaxed setting can move you into higher consciousness and into the trance state. The trance state is the NOW moment. This is the place where dreams are birthed and where we manifest our reality. This practice leads us to our next topic of meditation.

Meditation

During meditation we are able to connect with higher vibrational states of consciousness, otherworldly beings and commune with our higher self. The very outer realm of meditation is very helpful for people who are not even into advanced spirituality, trance states or metaphysics. Meditation is very helpful for any person of any religion or creed to release stress and tension by focusing on their breathing and clearing their mind.

Music

Music is also a great way to stimulate your third eye. Bin-aural beats are an excellent way to enter into trance state. Listening to bin-aural beats will cause the brain to resonate in tune with that beat and in turn produce trance. Hearing drums in any song can put you into a higher vibratory state. Tribal drums and anything heard in rhythm can initiate these higher states of consciousness. I enjoy listening to different tones. There are particular tones that do different things for you. Some tones take you even more quickly into the trance state when you raise your vibrational frequency to the same pitch as the tones by concentrating and focusing on them. Tibetan singing bowls also produce a loud musical vibratory note. These notes resonate to the very core of your consciousness and can help you awaken and arise to that trance state or state of higher consciousness. I find the singing bowls very helpful for clearing the air around you and clearing your body of negative frequencies which act as a barrier to connecting to the spirit world through your third eye.

Part 7
Entering The Trance State

Burning Incense

Burning incense is a great way to put you into a more relaxed state. There are certain aromas that stimulate parts of the brain for relaxation, sleep, memory and other cognitive functions. I particularly like to burn copal resin, which was used by the ancient Mayans before entering trance-state and performing rituals. Burning sage and Palo Santo wood are also used for clearing an area of negative energies and are very sacred practices. Your brain essentially associates the smell of these aromas with cleansing, and allows a faster way into the spirit realm. These practices will work well for you in stimulating your third eye (pineal gland) and becoming more acquainted with operating within the spiritual dimensions. These techniques will cause your intuition to sharpen and also increase synchronicities in your life.

Synchronicity

Synchronicity is a word that was coined by Carl Jung. This word is used when referring to the experience of having two unrelated occurrences that that seem to be meaningfully connected. People report hearing phrases and seeing number sequences multiple times within the same day that seem to stand out as significant, but are only noted as coincidences. A lot of people experience this each time they look at a clock and the numbers read in multiples like 3:33, 4:44, 5:55, and 11:11. Synchronicities seem to almost be breadcrumbs from the Creator letting us know that we are on the right path. Along with aligning number sequences, people report that they have seemed to step into some type of energetic flow with the universe where these patterns are not only happening with numbers but through everything in their life. Doors open to the person and manifestations seem to happen in their life with little or no effort. Things that the individual is thinking about seem to appear with ease when they step into this union flow with the universe. Christians have referred to this as being in the perfect will of God and have also referred to it as confirmation. A daily routine of spiritual practice seems to be the best way to maintain this balance and bring about synchronicities into your life.

Once you start going deeper within the Biblical mysteries, you will find out about ancient truths that were once practiced and believed by the early church. These truths seem to reiterate themselves through the scriptures but remain hidden to those who only approach the Bible from a literal view point. The strange thing is that the more you study you end up finding these truths are evident throughout many ancient religions of antiquity. This usually leads to the study of syncretism and finding out the similarities within the majority of religious doctrines. Although names and titles may change from book to book, there is an essence that remains constant throughout the spiritual and allegorical interpretations of the texts. This is what the early Essenes and Gnostic groups believed, that we must first cater to the inside of man and his spiritual life to be able to bring order to the minute things we face on the outside in our day to day lives. Renew the mind and the rest will follow. The early Christians believed strongly in spiritual manifestations of many kinds and these manifestations were a part of their daily lives. When we compare this ideology and lifestyle with those of the Tao, Hermeticism or any other faiths or beliefs, we then begin to find common ground. This is a necessity if we are going to progress together. As above so below. As within so without.

Part 7
Entering The Trance State

PART 8
Elemental Spirits

Elemental spirit beings were described in the 16th century through the work of Paracelsus as being entities associated with the four elements of Earth, Water, Air and Fire. Some circles add a fifth element of ether or spirit to the list. Each of the named elements are said to have beings that work to ensure that nature and their appropriate elemental kingdoms works properly. This could be the filtration of the oceans and pulling of tides, assisting plants and vegetation in their growth, the blowing of the wind and cool breeze or the purification properties of fire. For Earth you have the Gnomes, Water has Undines, Air has Sylphs and Fire has the Salamanders. These beings are said to be invisible to human eyes, but throughout ancient lore people have claimed to have caught a glimpse of them. These beings have also been mistaken for or called by other names such as Fairies, Pixies, Elves, Leprechauns, Trolls, Newts and other creatures associated

Völuspá (1895) by Lorenz Frølich

with the elemental kingdoms. Although most people cite not being able to see these beings, many feel their presence. In folklore some of these beings are said to be playful, mischievous tricksters. From hiding car keys to misplacing socks, many attribute these strange

Part 8
Elemental Spirits

occurrences to the work of elemental beings. In times past the knowledge of the elemental spirits and beings were only passed down throughout folklore and embedded within literature. In present day, Hollywood has done a fantastic job portraying them in films, allowing new generations to embrace the mystique and wonder of nature spirits. Video games such as World of Warcraft and countless others also have a great bit of information in them about nature beings and the spirits of the ethers and their magick.

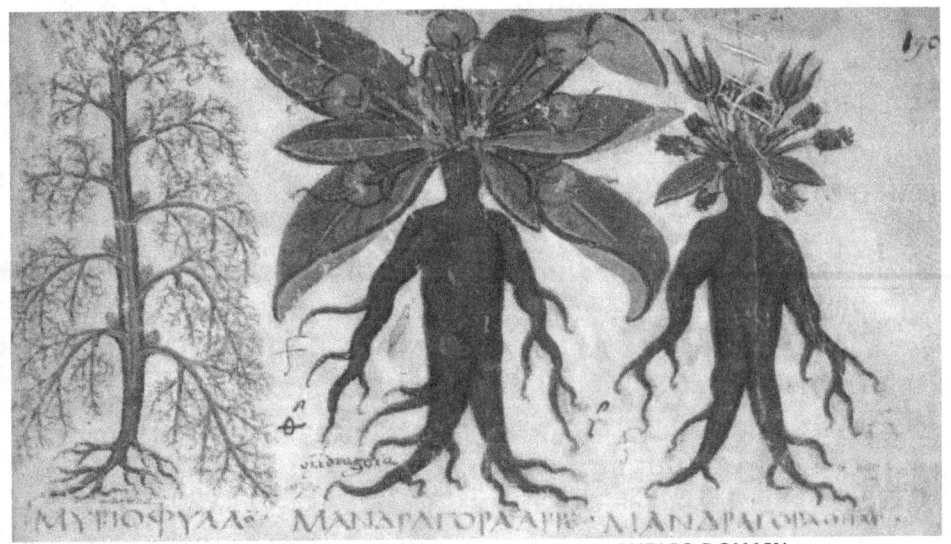

Mandrakes from a 7th century manuscript. PUBLIC DOMAIN

Madam Blavatsky writes that there are different sects in the order of the elemental kingdoms, distinctively The Elements, Elementals and Elementaries. These beings can be created or summoned, yet they are not eternal. Once these beings serve their purpose they die and that is the end of them.

"The creatures evolved in the four kingdoms of Earth, Air, Fire and Water, and called by the kabalists gnomes, sylphs, salamanders, and undines. They may be termed the forces of nature and will either operate effects as the servile agents of general law or may be employed by the disembodied - whether pure or impure - and by living adepts of magic and sorcery, to produce desired phenomenal results. Such beings never become men. Under the general designation fairies, and feys, these spirits of the Elements appear in the myth, fable, tradition or poetry of all nations, ancient and modern. Their names are legion - peris, devs, djins, sylvans, satyrs, fauns, elves, dwarfs, trolls, norns, nisses, kobolds, brownies, necks, stromkals, undines, nixes, salamanders, goblins, ponkes, banshees, kelpies, pixies, moss people, good people, good neighbours, wild women, men of peace, white ladies - and many more. They have been seen, feared, blessed, banned, and invoked, in every quarter of the globe and in every age. Shall we then concede that all who have met them were hallucinated?" | Isis Unveiled - Helena Petrovna Blavatsky

In parts of the Bible where we read about God speaking to humans, it is interesting to note that on many occasions he allowed angels to communicate through the elements on His behalf. The angel of the Lord communicated with Moses through a burning bush. In Judges 13:20 the angel of the Lord appears to speak with Manoah and upon his departure enters back into the fire to ascend back into the heavens. Knowing that the word angel only means messenger, could it be that these prophets were communicating with elemental spirits? Many in occult circles practice a form of fire gazing, in which they believe they are able to communicate with beings within the flames. Sometimes they see pictures, faces or receive messages telepathically. The smoke and ashes are also held sacred and can be used. In yogic tradition, many practices a form of fire gazing where they stare at the flame of a candle and concentrate on it with their minds eye. This practice is said to increase psychic abilities as they bring the fires energy to the third eye chakra.

Part 8
Elemental Spirits

Fairy Encounter

John Duncan (1886 – 1945, Scottish)

I've personally had a beautiful encounter with my daughter with what I believe were Fairies or Pixies. Sometime after building a fairy house in our backyard, we were stargazing and spending time in nature. All of a sudden, these little florescent blue lights began to appear just above us in the tree line. I jokingly said "Those are fairies!" and we asked them to come down. Well, they did. The little blue orbs seemed to be around three to four inches long and were very beautiful. The lights came down just above our heads and they began to encircle me and my daughter. As beautiful and magical as it was, just as quick as they came down they in turn ascended back into the tree line and back into the forest. The experience was magical. We then went back inside to tell my wife what we experienced then I immediately got online to try and google blue fireflies to no avail. I didn't find anything online that was similar in any way to what we had just experienced.

Spirit Realm: Angels, Demons, Spirits and the Sovereignty of God

Elemental Spirits and Golems

Many of us have heard of the term Golem from J.R.R. Tolkien's *The Lord of The Rings*. As I mentioned before, Hollywood has done a great job embodying some of these ancient spiritual mysteries.

The word Golem is mentioned only once in the Bible in Psalm 139:16 saying:
YOUR EYES SAW MY UNFORMED BODY (GOLEM); ALL THE DAYS ORDAINED FOR ME WERE WRITTEN IN YOUR BOOK BEFORE ONE OF THEM CAME TO BE.

A Golem is a being that is formed out of the elements and then by way of magical enchantment or spell is brought to life. Essentially it is a body formed without a soul.

In Jewish lore on a few occasions rabbis have created Golems out of mud and by a few different means were able to bring them to life. Some say that one way to bring them to life is to write the Hebrew name of God on its forehead and to kill it one must remove the letters. Others say that you need to walk in a circle around the lifeless form and chant the secret names of God

Il golem e il rabbino Jehuda Löw in un disegno di Mikoláš Aleš (1899)

to bring it to life and walk counter clockwise to destroy it. Other sources say once the Golem has been physically

Part 8
Elemental Spirits

made, one needed to write the letters aleph, mem, tav, which is emet and means 'truth,' on the Golem's forehead and the Golem would come alive. Erase the aleph and you are left with mem and tav, which is met meaning 'death.' Jewish lore goes on to record the fact that Rabbi Judah Loew ben Bezalel, the Maharal of Prague, was able to successfully create and bring to life a Golem creature who was able to protect the city and do physical labor because Golems are very strong. If left alive too long, legend says that the Golem usually goes mad and begins to terrorize the community. Are Golems real or just the production of an overactive imagination and wishful thinking? We are created in the image and likeness of a creator God and when we create we are acting just like our father. Give us a tree, we will create a chair. Give us stones, we will create tools. God has placed within the us ingenuity and the ability to create art, and with the use of both mankind has evolved into what we are today. But what about life, can we create life? We can procreate but do we have the ability to breathe life into another? This in essence is what the scripture calls prophesying, the ability to speak to the winds to breathe life into an individual, circumstance or situation, but what about matter? Can we create matter? Can we create a mountain? We can paint pictures of mountains but can we create them? Are there limitations on how much authority we have as humans in this realm? Do we work within certain parameters governed by God? It is said that Adam was a form of a Golem, being crafted out of the dirt and remaining lifeless until God breathed the breath of life into his nostrils to create mankind. There are many other cultures with similar stories of creatures like the Golem. Robots and Frankenstein are two notable character types which get their conception from the Jewish Golem.

Attacked by an Elemental Shade

Much like the Golem, it is said that people can summon spirits to bring about their bidding on the earth. There are spells and incantations that people (notably witches and warlocks) perform to cast protection spells on their belongings or help them retrieve lost items etc. Some magicians are said to be able to create these types of entities out of the elements by the use of smoke. These entities can appear as a mist, gas or shadow beings as well. Many in the dark arts have worked with these types of spirits to cause harm or send ill will towards an unsuspecting person in the form of a curse or hex. I have personally had an encounter with a warlock who summoned an elemental spirit upon me.

While we were teenagers my girlfriend Arien and I were studying black magic and the occult, and we were limited when it came to the books that were available. We had a lot of them. We would walk into any book store wearing our biggest baggiest clothes to get as many books as we could and shove them into our clothes to steal them, but just reading the book was not nearly as effective as talking to a teacher or someone with experience. That's were Pops came in. Pops was a friend of ours. He was in his late 30's and lived in a trailer park close to Arien's house. All of the neighborhood teenagers hung out at Pops' house. We all sat around drinking, smoking pot and playing video games the majority of the time. Almost every single day was like a huge party. He was a Warlock. He knew everything there was to know about the craft, so we were in luck. Pops would tell us anything we wanted to know. We would sit over there and drink and get high and ask him all the questions we could think of and he would always know the answers. We stayed up all night talking to him and would usually end up crashing on the couch. One year, I was living in Louisiana and for my birthday I asked my mom to

Part 8
Elemental Spirits

drop me off in Alabama to be with Arien for a week. We picked up my cousin Alan from Atmore first. Then, we went to Saraland. We had a place to stay at a friend's house for two days. Before we left their house, I knew I was leaving back to Louisiana in a couple of days, so I stole from my friends and filled my tote bag with all the cool stuff I could get my hands on. I stole CD's, clothes, video games and controllers. We had to leave there after two days and went to the next friend's house, where we stayed for two more days and stole even more stuff. My cousin and I waited for my Mom to come get me, but day after day she never showed up. I stayed with all the friends I could think of, but their generosity ran out and I had a tote bag filled with all of their belongings. I stashed my bag at my friend Daniel's house, but I had stolen stuff from him too. Pops lived right across the street, so we hung out over there and stayed with him for about two days. We finally talked to my mom and she was supposed to show up the next day to pick us up, so we decided to steal a Dungeons and Dragons video game from Pops. We got the game and walked next door to Daniel's house and put it in my tote bag. By that time we had acquired a lot of stuff. Then we walked back to Pops' house and we were hanging out. Mom delayed again and was going to be a couple of more days because of car troubles, so we tried to stay at Pops' for a few more days till she came. One afternoon we were sitting on the couch in a room full of people, some I knew and some I didn't know. Our friend Stevo walked through the door with the Dungeons and Dragons video game in his hands that we had stolen from Pops the day before. Alan didn't notice it, but my heart stopped. I was really scared, and there were all of these big guys there wearing all black who I had never met. Pops looked at one of the guys next to him and they shook their heads and whispered something to Stevo. They then got up and walked to the back of the house one at a time. I immediately got up and walked over to Alan and told him we had to leave NOW! He didn't want to because they were about to start drinking and smoking pot and there were a bunch of young girls there, but I sternly whispered, "DUDE LET'S GO." We walked outside and I told him what I had seen. I felt like we had to get out of there because most of the people there were involved in gang activity and I knew the situation would turn ugly FAST. There were a lot of people outside that I didn't know, so we walked up to some dude in a car who had a lot of people hanging around him and I said, "Dude, we need ride bad." So he gave us a ride down the street. I used his cell phone to call Arien because we were stranded in Creola with nowhere to go. We went over to her house where she said we could try to sneak and stay in her tree house. The guy who gave us a lift dropped us off down the street because Arien's parents wouldn't be cool with us staying over there. Alan and I walked a long way and hid in the bushes close to Arien's house. We were waiting for the right moment to run to the tree house. While we waited, it started to get dark. We saw a light behind her house that looked like someone walking around with a flashlight, but we didn't see any person, just an eerie light floating around and back and forth. We watched the light for about an hour thinking that her dad was walking around with a flashlight. We tried to avoid the light and walked to the other side of the bushes where there was an open field that went around to the back of her house. We went around and as soon as we got in the open, something appeared out of thin air that looked like a huge camel that was eight feet tall and made out of the blackest night! The creature came running at us! Alan and I both saw it and both of us were knocked to the ground as it screamed and ran by before vanishing into thin air. We were both dazed and completely freaked out as we got up and ran as fast as we could to Arien's tree house. We finally made it. Arien and her friend Wendi came to stay the night up there with us. We later found out that Pops had a protection spell on his belongings. That means that if someone steals something

Part 8
Elemental Spirits

of his, the spirits would track the stuff down and actually track the thieves down to return the belongings. These spirits are known as elementals and they are manifested into our reality by being summoned though earth, air, fire, water or spirit.

You would think that an experience like this would run someone far away from anything demonic or of the occult, but not me. It lit a fire in me and I wanted to know more. I knew that if I could get good enough then I could learn to summon spirits for myself. This sucked me in even deeper and eventually led me to demonic possession.

Eventually I ended up back in Louisiana after my mom finally showed up to get me. There I spent a lot of time in our trailer in the woods alone in the middle of nowhere. Those spirits continued to harass me for a long time. Sometimes I would be sitting at home alone waiting for my mom to get home around midnight. While sitting on the couch inside our trailer, the wind started blowing and I heard soft whispering voices like in the movies, only I couldn't understand what they were saying. It was like a few people whispering secrets to each other.

Spirit Realm: Angels, Demons, Spirits and the Sovereignty of God

Orobas" in: Collin de Plancy (1863) Dictionnaire Infernal

"The Christians call them "devils," "imps of Satan," and like characteristic names. They are nothing of the kind, but simply creatures of ethereal matter, irresponsible, and neither good nor bad, unless influenced by a superior intelligence." | Isis Unveiled - Helena Petrovna Blavatsky

Part 8
Elemental Spirits

Part 9
Symbols, Signs & Sigils

Symbols in and of themselves are said to hold no power. Beauty is in the eye of the beholder. Learning the meaning of symbols allows us to connect our consciousness to the ideas held within them and to embody them in our lives. Many people are able to look at the same sign or symbol and interpret different meanings. From their perspective the symbol means something totally different than it means to you. This also applies to words and terms. Much of the symbolism used today is only understood by those who are studied or initiated into that particular order. Looking at the back of paper money we see tons of symbolism. The all seeing eye, an eagle grasping thirteen arrows with his left talon and an olive branch in his right are depicted. There are also pyramids and the strange Latin words "*Novus ordo Seclorum*" and "*Annuit Coeptis*". Symbolism is a huge part of our lives and is used to communicate messages and wisdom to those who understand. Driving through the suburbs, one can pass by many buildings and overpasses with strange graffiti. To those on the outside it may look like weird art or even scribble, but those initiated into gang culture clearly see marked territory for a particular gang in these symbols with intricate meanings. Such is the same with Masonic orders and other religious sects.

Many people think that the five pointed star or pentagram is a demonic symbol

Part 9
Symbols, Signs & Sigils

when in fact it was used in antiquity to protect one from demonic and negative energies. Many will note that a symbol near and dear to Catholic faith is the upside down cross which is portrayed on many of their elaborate churches, garments and art. To the unlearned this symbol appears to be demonic, because in symbology when you invert a positive symbol you are changing its meaning to a negative. Unbeknownst to many when the upside down cross is used in Catholicism it represents the death of Saint Peter, who requested to be crucified upside down because he felt unworthy to die in the same manner as Jesus Christ. Catholics hold to the belief that the apostle Peter was the first Pope and founder of the Catholic faith. The upside down cross is also often used in Satanism to mock Christ and the Christian faith. The same is used with Pentagram, as flipping it upside down creates the Baphomet used by many Satanists to represent the dark lord. These two symbols are examples of creating the reverse effect of the symbol. Again, wisdom is to those who are learned.

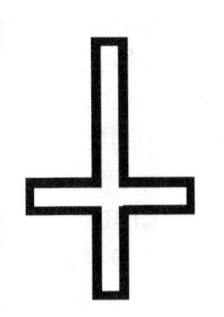

Symbols are very near and dear to our hearts. They serve as a reminder of a belief or a special moment in life. The cross necklace to the Christian reminds them of the saving grace of Jesus. The Bible is also held in high regard and both are embraced in a time of fear to bring about peace and faith in that situation. I have also seen both items used in exorcisms. These items hold no special significance in and of themselves, but they evoke faith and courage in the beholder. Tattoos also serve in like manner. People will get the images or names of their past loved ones tattooed on them and others their favorite Bible verse or super hero. These tattoos convey to us something meaningful which we would like to be reminded of often.

In the Bible, the children of Israel were commanded to wear mezuzahs around their neck and place them on the doorposts of their homes to be a reminder of God's blessing. There were other times in scripture when God did a miracle by providing supernaturally for the Israelites or when they overcame an enemy that they would build a monument. This monument also served as a reminder of these great feats. These monuments were usually piles of rocks or statues that each time they passed they were reminded of particular victories and covenants. Some believe that the Great Pyramid of Giza was created as a monument unto Yahweh and believe the following scripture as biblical proof from this concept.

IN THAT DAY THERE WILL BE AN ALTAR TO THE LORD IN THE HEART OF EGYPT, AND A MONUMENT TO THE LORD AT ITS BORDER. IT WILL BE A SIGN AND WITNESS TO THE LORD ALMIGHTY IN THE LAND OF EGYPT. WHEN THEY CRY OUT TO THE LORD BECAUSE OF THEIR OPPRESSORS, HE WILL SEND THEM A SAVIOR AND DEFENDER, AND HE WILL RESCUE THEM. | ISAIAH 19:19-20

In America, we have the Statue of Liberty in New York that was given to the U.S. by the French to represent freedom and liberty. The same is conveyed through Holy Days (Holidays). These feasts and festivities are held yearly such as birthdays, Easter, and Christmas. All serve as a reminder of different events and a time of rejoicing with the community. Many state flags and city emblems represent something special about that community that sets them apart from the rest.

Part 9
Symbols, Signs & Sigils

In the New Testament, Jesus commands his followers to partake of Holy Communion each time that they come together. Jesus says "This do in remembrance of me" knowing that they would need to be reminded daily. Elijah saw God do many miracles through his own hands and saw the divine work through many supernatural means, yet he fell into a dark depression sometime after. It is strange how the human mind works and how easily we forget. Signs and symbols serve a unique purpose in our lives helping to keep us conscious and living in the moment while reminding us who we are. I believe this is also like faith, because we often look at the situations and circumstances around us and find it so easy to lose hope when things appear rough. Faith reminds us along with the use of symbols that what God has done in the past He can and will do again in the future.

HOPE DEFERRED MAKETH THE HEART SICK: BUT WHEN THE DESIRE COMETH, IT IS A TREE OF LIFE. | PROVERBS 13:12

The Teraphim

Teraphim, from Athanasius Kircher, Oedipus Aegyptiacus, 1652

A Teraphim was a type of family idol or god that was crafted by Micah in the Bible in the form of a statue. Many believe that they were used as a medium for healing and it was said that a being from the other side had the ability to communicate through them. These Teraphim worked like a magical talisman as used by those in occult circles and was used as a form of divination. Many use the enchanted emblems and sigils engraved with esoteric markings on them to communicate with angelic beings as described by way of *Chaos Magick*.

As cited in the Testament of Solomon, Solomon was given a ring by the angel Michael that gave him the ability to command authority over demons. The engraving on the ring was that of a five pointed star, which served as a symbol of protection and is still used by many who practice spirit summoning to this day. Before rituals, many witches and magicians would draw a pentagram on the ground with the use of rocks, chalk or salt. It is believed that this magical symbol given to Solomon from God has the ability to protect the practitioner from any outside forces, actually consecrating the area readying it to performing magical rites.

Part 9
Symbols, Signs & Sigils

Cursed Objects

A cursed object is an object that is said to be cursed, carrying with it an omen with the intention of causing harm to anyone who may touch or come into possession of the item. During the ritual the person carrying out the deed may summon a demon or poltergeist to follow the object. In return, the person may offer blood or a sacrifice to the entity as a payment for their services rendered. Some people report being in homes that are haunted or cursed claiming to see images of ghostly figures within vanity mirrors or other objects. Many occultists use what are known as "Black Mirrors" to communicate with beings from the ethers as a form of scrying. The word scrying is from the Middle English word 'descry', which means 'to divine'. Scrying was most commonly done by crystal gazing. When you gaze at a shiny or blank surface, it is believed to open up the door to the subconscious mind that taps into extra-sensory perceptions.

Blessed Objects

If these beliefs and practices have any validity, then the opposite would in turn hold true. Just as there are cursed objects it is also believed that an object can be blessed and bring about good luck. Many believe that carrying the foot of a rabbit in their pocket brings about good luck, as well as finding a four leaf clover brings about luck and fortune. One legend says that horseshoes are lucky because they were traditionally made of iron. Mischievous fairies could not stand the touch of iron, so they shied away from houses that were adorned with it. Another legend attributes lucky horseshoes to Saint Dunstan, a historical figure who died in 988 AD. According to the legend, Dunstan, who was a blacksmith, was commanded by the devil to shoe his horse. Instead, Dunstan nailed a horseshoe to the devil's foot and refused to remove it and ease the devil's pain until he received a guarantee that the devil would stay away from any house with a horseshoe above the threshold of the door.

Christianity holds to the belief that water and anointing oils can be blessed by a Holy man or priest to rid one of ailments or evil spirits.

In Numbers chapter 5, we read about what is known as "The Test for an Unfaithful Wife". The test was demonstrated in this way. If a man had the suspicion that his wife had sexual relations outside of their marriage and had not been faithful, he was supposed to bring her to the priest and perform the ritual of the Sotah. The priest would make a magical elixir and have the woman drink it. The text reads as follows:

"IF NO OTHER MAN HAS HAD SEXUAL RELATIONS WITH YOU AND YOU HAVE NOT GONE ASTRAY AND BECOME IMPURE WHILE MARRIED TO YOUR HUSBAND, MAY THIS BITTER WATER THAT BRINGS A CURSE NOT HARM YOU. BUT IF YOU HAVE GONE ASTRAY WHILE MARRIED TO YOUR HUSBAND AND YOU HAVE MADE YOURSELF IMPURE BY HAVING SEXUAL RELATIONS WITH A MAN OTHER THAN YOUR HUSBAND (HERE THE PRIEST IS TO PUT THE WOMAN UNDER THIS CURSE) 'MAY THE LORD CAUSE YOU TO BECOME A CURSE AMONG YOUR PEOPLE WHEN HE MAKES YOUR WOMB MISCARRY AND YOUR ABDOMEN SWELL. MAY THIS WATER THAT BRINGS A CURSE ENTER YOUR BODY SO THAT YOUR ABDOMEN SWELLS OR YOUR WOMB MISCARRIES.' THEN THE WOMAN IS TO SAY, 'AMEN. SO BE IT.'" NUMBER 5:19-23

The priest would then write these curses on a scroll and then wash them off into the elixir of bitters and have the woman drink it. Was this really a magical elixir? Were there any reports of a woman drinking this concoction and having this happen to them? What may have been more than likely was that the woman would be too afraid to carry out the ritual would most likely admit of her wrong doing and confess before the priest.

It is also believed that items such as clothing could be blessed and carry healing powers from angelic forces or the anointing from God Himself. We have seen many televangelists selling their overpriced bottles of holy water or even pieces of cloth that they have blessed for a fee. Where does this practice come from? In Acts chapter 19 we read about the apostle Paul who was going around performing many miracles and healing all those who were sick. The text reads,

GOD DID EXTRAORDINARY MIRACLES THROUGH PAUL, SO THAT EVEN HANDKERCHIEFS AND APRONS THAT HAD TOUCHED HIM WERE TAKEN TO THE SICK, AND THEIR ILLNESSES WERE CURED AND THE EVIL SPIRITS LEFT THEM. ACTS 19:11-12

This is also similar to Jesus and the woman with the issue of blood in Matthew 19:20, where the woman reached out by faith to grab Jesus. She was only able to grab the hem of his robe yet she was healed.

Crystals

Crystals have been used for thousands of years and are believed to be able to harness energy and have magical properties. Quartz crystals are used inside of radios because they are able to dial in on the radio frequencies transmitted through the air via the antenna. These sound waves can then be amplified and heard with the use of a speaker. Crystals are also used to harness and expel electromagnetic frequencies. Different types of crystals produce specific types of vibrational resonance and are used for different things. Some people claim that specific crystals harness the power to heal and have calming properties, while others are able to block out harmful electromagnetic frequencies. Moldavite is a crystal formed by meteorite impact, some even date as far back as fifteen million years. Moldavite promotes spiritual growth, healing and psychic protection. Some would classify these claims as hogwash, but some very interesting studies have been done that seem to support such claims. One thing that is for sure is that the ancient Israelite priests knew the power of such stones.

Ephod

The Levite priest wore a breastplate used as a tool for divination and communicating with God. The breastplate was closely connected with oracular practices and priestly rituals. The breastplate was ordered to have twelve stones upon it and each jewel was engraved with the name of each tribe according to which stone the tribe was given. When worn, the Ephod had the ability to change the vibration of the priest to a higher frequency, readying him for an encounter with Yahweh. Many sects of kings and priest still use types of magical ephods today. The crown worn by kings is laden with many of the same crystals used on the

Part 9
Symbols, Signs & Sigils

ephod, hence making the crown a type of ephod for the head.

There are some discrepancies concerning the list of stones given to the twelve tribes but the most agreed upon are as follows:

> Levi: Carbuncle (red garnet)
> Zebulon: Diamond
> Gad: Amethyst
> Benjamin: Jasper
> Simeon: Chrysolite
> Issachar: Sapphire
> Naphtali: Agate
> Joseph: Onyx
> Reuben: Sard
> Judah: Emerald
> Dan: Topaz
> Asher: Beryl

Magical Staffs

The scepters carried by kings and priest today also hold magical crystals on the end that are known to possess power. The scepter or wand is used when performing rites and ceremonies still to this day. Aaron and Moses both had magical staffs in the Bible.

Along with crystals, God also gave each of the leaders of the twelve tribes staffs or rods that had the name of the correlating tribe engraved upon it. It was said of Aaron's rod that it 'put forth buds, produced blossoms, and bore ripe almonds'.

During a showdown between Moses, Aaron and Pharaoh's two Sorcerers Jannes and Jambres, Aaron threw down his

Spirit Realm: Angels, Demons, Spirits and the Sovereignty of God

staff and it became a snake. Pharaoh's magicians by enchantment and magick threw theirs down and mimicked what Aaron had done, also turning their rods into snakes. Yet, during the duel Aaron's serpent devoured the other. Aaron's rod is again used to turn the Nile into blood. It is also used several times on God's command to initiate the plagues of Egypt.

During the exodus Moses raises his staff to part the Red Sea for the Israelites to escape Egypt. Moses also used his staff to strike a rock that created a spring of water for the Israelites to drink from in the wilderness.

Bible Pictures" book, by W. A. Foster, 1897

Part 9
Symbols, Signs & Sigils

Spirit Realm: Angels, Demons, Spirits and the Sovereignty of God

PART 10
DIVINATION

Paris 1888, for Flammarion's 1888 L'atmosphère : météorologie populaire

Divination has an answer from the divine for every situation. There are many forms of divination such as tea leaf readings, cleromancy i.e. the rolling of special dice and the pulling of straws. The term divination immediately brings up a red flag for most Christians because it was something that was forbidden in the Bible. Upon further study we find that the act of divination was used many times throughout the Bible as something righteous and was used to determine the will of God by the

Part 10
Divination

prophets and disciples. They used an ancient form of divination called "The Casting of Lots". Casting lots was a method used by the Jews of the Old Testament and by the Christian disciples to determine the will of God. Lots could be sticks with markings, stones with symbols etc. These lots were thrown into a small area and then the result was interpreted. This is where the term "The Luck of the Draw" comes from. Children also somewhat practice a form of luck when picking someone for a task such as 'Rock, Paper, Scissors' and 'Eenie Meenie Miney Mo'.

One of the main reasons divination is looked at as something negative is because in the New Testament in Acts chapter 16, there was a certain fortune teller that the scriptures says was possessed by the spirit of *Divination*. This woman would follow the Apostle Paul around mocking him and his ministry. Paul grew tiresome of her following and mocking and in turn rebuked the spirit that was within her. When he did this the spirit left and the woman lost her power to predict the future. The Greek word used here doesn't mean 'Divination' but '*Python*'. This is referring to the Pythian serpent that was said to have guarded the oracle at Delphi and known to have been slain by Apollo in Greek mythology. This woman was channeling the Pythian spirit and was able to predict the future and tell fortunes because of it's influence.

Divination by itself is not something bad or something to be afraid of. The prophets and disciples all participated in forms of divination and ritual in order to communicate with God. It is all about the intention and manner of which one uses this tool. In the case of the spirit of Python, the texts show us how people are able to channel foreign spirits in order to gain information about people and circumstances. In the end there is usually a high price to pay for this information.

Let's examine a few scriptures and examples within the Bible that seem to be overlooked when discussing this subject. When trying to understand the Casting of Lots, one of the key scriptures to note is Proverbs 16:33 which reads:

"THE LOT IS CAST INTO THE LAP, BUT ITS EVERY DECISION IS FROM THE LORD,"

This scripture plainly tells us that when the lot is cast that it is God himself who determines its very outcome.

Joshua casting lots for the tribes of Israel Author Unknown

Part 10
Divination

Jonah

In the story of Jonah and the whale, Jonah was running from God. He boarded a ship headed to Tarshish when he was supposed to be headed to Nineveh. The people of the ship ended up going through a dangerous storm and started to throw their personal cargo off of the ship so that it wouldn't capsize. In a panic the men began to ask everyone to cry out to their gods for help and the men found Jonah asleep in the bottom of the ship. Then the sailors said to each other, "**COME, LET US CAST LOTS TO FIND OUT WHO IS RESPONSIBLE FOR THIS CALAMITY.**" They cast lots and the lot fell on Jonah. (Jonah 1:7). It was God who sent the storm and through the casting of lots it was God who told the men that Jonah was the reason that the storm had come.

Joseph and Matthias

In the first chapter of the book of Acts, we see the disciples trying to move forward after the ascension of Jesus and the death of Judas. Standing with the now eleven disciples, Peter quotes a scripture from the book of Psalms which reads: "'May his place be deserted; let there be no one to dwell in it,' and, "'May another take his place of leadership". The disciples knew that they needed someone to take the place that Judas once held among the twelve and there were two men up for the position, Joseph and Matthias. They then prayed,

"**LORD, YOU KNOW EVERYONE'S HEART. SHOW US WHICH OF THESE TWO YOU HAVE CHOSEN TO TAKE OVER THIS APOSTOLIC MINISTRY, WHICH JUDAS LEFT TO GO WHERE HE BELONGS. THEN THEY CAST LOTS, AND THE LOT FELL TO MATTHIAS; SO HE WAS ADDED TO THE ELEVEN APOSTLES.**"

ACTS CHAPTER 1:20

This was another instance where the casting of lots was used to determine an outcome and this example is in the New Testament.

This next scripture also mentions using divination to determine the blessing from God:

BUT LABAN SAID TO HIM, "IF I HAVE FOUND FAVOR IN YOUR EYES, PLEASE STAY. I HAVE LEARNED BY DIVINATION THAT THE LORD HAS BLESSED ME BECAUSE OF YOU." HE ADDED, "NAME YOUR WAGES, AND I WILL PAY THEM." GENESIS 30:27-28

Genesis 44:15 is another really good one that reads:

JOSEPH SAID TO THEM, "WHAT IS THIS YOU HAVE DONE? DON'T YOU KNOW THAT A MAN LIKE ME CAN FIND THINGS OUT BY DIVINATION?"

Part 10
Divination

David Consulting the High Priest by the Urim and Thummim 1732

Urim and Thummin

The Urim and Thummin were believed to be two stones carried in a bag by the high priest specifically while wearing the ephod breastplate. When it came time to make a decision or seek the answer of a YES or NO question the high priest would reach into his bag and pull out one of the two stones to reveal what God would say about the matter. Some believed that the engravings etched into the stones would light up and vibrate determining the will of God. Urim and Thummin are Hebraic terms meaning Light and Complete Truth.

Intention

Just like with all spiritual practices, what makes something like divination or the casting of lots evil is the intention of the heart. Is it being used for malicious intent or to harm someone? Are you doing it to contact benevolent entities? Just like prayer and meditation, divination is simply a tool. It depends on the manner in which it is being used to determine if it is good or evil. When you pray, are you praying to fallen deities that they might come forth and cause someone harm? Or are you praying in communion with God and praying for the sick and afflicted to recover? When you meditate are you looking to channel and use your body as a vehicle to let dark energies come through? Or are you looking to channel God's heart and receive inspiration from The Holy Spirit? Divination was created by God for us to commune and seek His thought on a matter. There are many warnings throughout the Bible forbidding people to seek after those who consult with familiar spirits and fortune tellers. One of the main reasons is that many were lying about what they saw or lying about even being able to see at all. We still see a great deal of this today.

Part 10
Divination

Why seek after a lesser spirit or entity when we have direct access to the greatest of them all? There are many lying and seductive spirits masquerading in the ethers waiting to make pacts with humans to carry out their own evil desires. On the other hand, there are also beautiful spirits that interact directly with mankind as well. The problem is trying to consult them for information instead to going directly of God himself. This is why the scripture tells us to "Test the Spirits".

DEAR FRIENDS, DO NOT BELIEVE EVERY SPIRIT, BUT TEST THE SPIRITS TO SEE WHETHER THEY ARE FROM GOD | 1 JOHN 4:1

Some Christian ministries are starting to embrace the ancient practice of the casting of lots and they are seeing many breakthroughs with the use of this practice. I myself have used a deck of cards called the "Tarot of the Most High" in some of my personal sessions with clients. These tools work off of our own spiritual discernment through implementing the word of knowledge and wisdom.

"THE LOT IS CAST INTO THE LAP, BUT ITS EVERY DECISION IS FROM THE LORD," | PROVERBS 16:33

Spirit Realm: Angels, Demons, Spirits and the Sovereignty of God

PART 11
WHO IS LUCIFER?

The Fall of Lucifer, Gustave Doré, 1866

THY POMP IS BROUGHT DOWN TO THE GRAVE, AND THE NOISE OF THY VIOLS: THE WORM IS SPREAD UNDER THEE, AND THE WORMS COVER THEE. HOW ART THOU FALLEN FROM HEAVEN, O LUCIFER, SON OF THE MORNING! HOW ART THOU CUT DOWN TO THE GROUND, WHICH DIDST WEAKEN THE NATIONS!

Part 11
Who Is Lucifer?

FOR THOU HAST SAID IN THINE HEART, I WILL ASCEND INTO HEAVEN; I WILL EXALT MY THRONE ABOVE THE STARS OF GOD: I WILL SIT ALSO UPON THE MOUNT OF THE CONGREGATION, IN THE SIDES OF THE NORTH: I WILL ASCEND ABOVE THE HEIGHTS OF THE CLOUDS; I WILL BE LIKE THE MOST HIGH. YET THOU SHALT BE BROUGHT DOWN TO HELL, TO THE SIDES OF THE PIT. THEY THAT SEE THEE SHALL NARROWLY LOOK UPON THEE, AND CONSIDER THEE, SAYING, IS THIS THE MAN THAT MADE THE EARTH TO TREMBLE, THAT DID SHAKE KINGDOMS; | ISAIAH 14:11-16

Lucifer has to be one of the most misunderstood words in Christendom. In church we were told that Lucifer, Satan and The Devil are the same entities. Actually, Lucifer is only mentioned once in the Bible and it's not talking about the devil. When Lucifer is mentioned in Isaiah 14 it is being used as a title because the word Lucifer comes from the Latin origin meaning "light bearer". The first part of the word is "Luci" from the Latin *lux* or *lucis*, meaning "light" and the second part "Ferre" meaning "bringer" or "to carry". The reason this word is being used in this scripture is because this chapter is addressed to the king of Babylon as a prophecy or warning of his fate for enslaving Gods people. This chapter speaks not of the ambition and fall of Satan, but of the pride, arrogance, and fall of Nebuchadnezzar. There is also an analogy being used as the text says "O Lucifer, son of the Morning". This analogy is mocking the king of Babylon and basically saying that his fall would be like the fall of the planet Venus. Each morning as the stars and planets shine in all their glory the planet Venus is the brightest light in the morning sky until the rising of the Sun, and then Venus loses his seat thus being cast out of Heaven. In the text there is no mention of a Satan or a Devil, but verse 16 says plainly "**IS THIS THE MAN THAT MADE THE EARTH TO TREMBLE**", the key word being "man". The Bible is full of astrological references from Genesis to Revelation. It ranges from talking about the Zodiac to calling out Orion, Pleiades, and other constellations by their names.

The reason that most Christians associate the word Lucifer with Satan is because of the fall. Kings and gods were falling and being cast down all throughout the Bible. I've also heard many Christians say that Satan was the chief musician or worship leader in heaven. This is not true either. Many people connect dots that aren't even there, and we believe it just because it's what we were told and it becomes accepted as tradition. They get this from Ezekiel chapter 28 which is actually speaking about the King of Tyre.

Again, Satan is not God's enemy. Satan does not think that one day he will overthrow God and take His throne like we were told in Sunday school. In reality, Satan is OUR enemy. Revelation 12:10 refers to Satan as the accuser of the brethren when it says "**THE ACCUSER OF OUR BRETHREN IS CAST DOWN, WHICH ACCUSED THEM BEFORE OUR GOD DAY AND NIGHT**". This goes back to the book of Job showing the Satan figure appearing before God and bringing up accusations against Job. The word Satan means adversary and many people have played the role of a Satan much like the Apostle Peter. (See First Chapter)

Part 11
Who Is Lucifer?

Spirit Realm: Angels, Demons, Spirits and the Sovereignty of God

Part 12
Fasting To Rid One's Self of Spirits

A mediæval illustration of Jesus healing the Gerasene Public Domain

Part 12
Fasting To Rid One's Self of Spirits

In the study of deliverance from demons, whether corporate or personal, we must understand the power of fasting. In this chapter we will look at the importance of Biblically fasting and what it does for the body and spirit. There are a few key scriptures for us to examine. The first excerpt is a story in Matthew 17. In this chapter, a man approached Jesus with his son who was demon possessed and was continually throwing himself down into the water and fire. The man told Jesus that he had already brought his son to Jesus's disciples, but they could not heal him. After hearing this, Jesus seemed to get a little annoyed and replied,

"YOU UNBELIEVING AND PERVERSE GENERATION," JESUS REPLIED, "HOW LONG SHALL I STAY WITH YOU? HOW LONG SHALL I PUT UP WITH YOU? BRING THE BOY HERE TO ME." JESUS REBUKED THE DEMON, AND IT CAME OUT OF THE BOY, AND HE WAS HEALED AT THAT MOMENT. | MATTHEW 17:17-18

The disciples then asked Jesus why they couldn't heal the boy and Jesus said,

"BECAUSE YOU HAVE SO LITTLE FAITH. TRULY I TELL YOU, IF YOU HAVE FAITH AS SMALL AS A MUSTARD SEED, YOU CAN SAY TO THIS MOUNTAIN, 'MOVE FROM HERE TO THERE,' AND IT WILL MOVE. NOTHING WILL BE IMPOSSIBLE FOR YOU. | 17:20

The next verse is omitted from many Bible translations but is a very important doctrine which reads,

HOWBEIT THIS KIND GOETH NOT OUT BUT BY PRAYER AND FASTING. | 17:21

Jesus tells them that with just a little faith they are able to move mountains (strongholds) and then He goes on to say that there are certain demons are only cast out by prayer and fasting. Why is this? Some of these spirits must be starved out. If you continue to feed stray dogs around your home they will continue to come expecting to eat, but if you don't give the dog food eventually he will leave and find his meals elsewhere. Fasting does many things on many levels. Spiritually, it acts as a statement of faith letting God know that we are serious about a situation. It also helps us to focus on the weightier matters of the soul because our main thought and survival instinct is that we are hungry and need to be filled. Once we set that aside, we are able to go a little deeper into what our spirit actually needs to survive.

IT IS WRITTEN, "MAN SHALL NOT LIVE BY BREAD ALONE, BUT BY EVERY WORD THAT PROCEEDETH OUT OF THE MOUTH OF GOD." | MATTHEW 4:4

Isaiah chapter 58 is known as the true fast and holds some key information about fasting. Verse 6 reads

IS NOT THIS THE FAST THAT I HAVE CHOSEN? TO LOOSE THE BANDS OF WICKEDNESS, TO UNDO THE HEAVY BURDENS, AND TO LET THE OPPRESSED GO FREE, AND THAT YE BREAK EVERY YOKE?

This is another key scripture that shines a light on why some demons only leave through prayer and fasting. It says that the fast is to "loose the bands of wickedness". This band is something that "binds" you, and in this case it is when you are bound to wickedness or habitual sins. If you find yourself stuck in a rut and continually repeating the same scenarios over and over again in your life, try fasting. The scripture also goes on to say that fasting is a way to "undo heavy burdens and to let the oppressed go free, and break every yoke". This statement is also echoed by Jesus when he states "**COME TO ME, ALL YOU WHO ARE WEARY AND BURDENED, AND I WILL GIVE YOU REST. TAKE MY YOKE UPON YOU AND LEARN FROM ME, FOR I AM GENTLE AND HUMBLE IN HEART, AND YOU WILL FIND REST FOR YOUR**

Part 12
Fasting To Rid One's Self of Spirits

SOULS. FOR MY YOKE IS EASY AND MY BURDEN IS LIGHT." | MATTHEW 11:28-30

Many times if we are looking to get out of a cycle of self-abuse or sin we must lay down the bad habit, but also pick up a new one. Many people who are trying to quit smoking start chewing gum. I've also seen people carrying pencils because they are so use to having something in their hand. Jesus tells us to take His yoke upon us and learn from Him because His yoke is easy and His burden is light. A yoke is a band or bond that is usually a wooden beam used between a pair of oxen or other animals to enable them to pull together on a load when working in pairs. There is strength in numbers and Jesus is beckoning us to partner and link in with him. He will help us carry the load. Many times we are carrying loads that we weren't intended to carry in the first place.

Parasites and Dragons

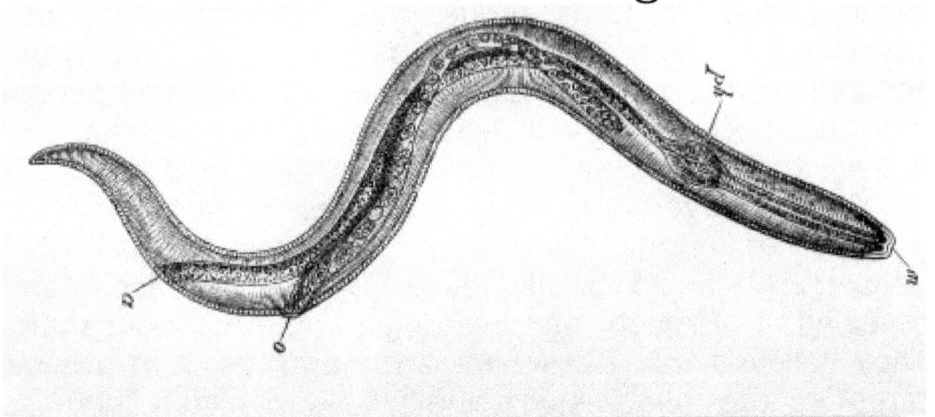

There is another side to fasting that is more physical and practical, but it is still a mirror image to the spiritual realm. When fasting for long periods of time, the body goes through a process where it purges itself of unhealthy bacteria and toxins. Fasting also acts as a cleanse and is being embraced by many doctors, nutritionists and health experts today as an easy way to flush the body from these stagnate toxins. Many people even report strange odors while the toxins are being released and parasites in their stool. The stomach, which is also called our second brain, plays a huge role in the way we feel and how our entire body is functioning. The body is a huge eco system full of living parasites coexisting together within us. Some are healthy and some are not. Some act as foreign enemies and others as guardians of the holy temple. There is an entire world or universe happening within and on us at all times. These microscopic organisms, bacteria and parasites are even fighting a holy war unknown to most people. This is mirrored in the spirit realm. There are spirits, angels and demons all at war around us on a daily basis. Many of these demons or unclean spirits act as parasites leeching energy off of their host. Just like in the physical where you would need a trained eye or microscopic lens to see these parasites, the same works for the spirit. One who is trained in the spirit or has sharpened the use of their third eye can feel when these entities are present, and in many cases even see them. When unhealthy parasites get into the body, they can cause the person to become very sick or even die. Spiritually when unclean spirits drain their host, the person can also become very ill leaving their host psychotic. I believe that this is the reason that Jesus would go into a city and heal everyone there. He understood sickness to be a "spirit of infirmity" and would cast the spirits out of people. The ancients also believed in this concept and revealed it through their writings and renaissance art. They believed that the worms and parasites were a huge threat to the human body and usually depicted them as great dragons. There are even prayers and spells to ward the body from this pestilence.

Part 12
Fasting To Rid One's Self of Spirits

Here is a Saxon prayer dating back to the 9th Century in Germany;

"Contra Vermes" (Against Worms)

Go out, worm, with nine wormlings,
out of the marrow into the bone,
from that bone into the flesh,
out from the flesh into the skin,
out from that skin into this arrow.
Lord, so Will it BE! "
By out no matter in insects, nine animals of microfilariae us,
From the bone marrow into the bone, and from bone to meat,
From meat to the skin, from the skin to this arrow.
Lord, it Shimeyo become emergency so!

The next topic in fasting for us to explore is called the Daniel fast. This fast contains nuts, fruits, vegetables and water only. This is another great way to flush the body of toxins and impurities. We have two examples for Daniel's fast and his set apart diet concerning the body. The first is in Daniel chapter 1 where Daniel and a few others refused to eat from the kings table. While the King fed his servants wine, meats and delicacies, Daniel and his friends ate only vegetables. After ten days of testing, Daniel and his friends appeared to be in better health than all the king's servants who had been eating from the king's table. The scripture even goes on to say in Daniel 1:17 that Daniel and his three friends had excelled in wisdom past any of the king's magicians and astrologers. God gave knowledge and understanding of all kinds of literature and learning to Daniel and his men. It is believed that when the body is spending less time processing heavy foods and breaking down meats that our cognitive abilities function more effectively, hence the gut being the second mind. There is an old adage that says "garbage in, garbage out", which holds true in this teaching.

Another example we have from Daniel is found in Daniel chapter 10. In this chapter Daniel goes on a three week fast where he ate no pleasant food, no meat and no wine. At the end of the three weeks Daniel is granted a vision where an angelic being is sent to him. Daniel was the only one who was able to see the being, but great fear fell upon the men who were with him and they all fled to hide themselves. In the vision the angel speaks with Daniel about the secrets of prayer and the course of specific angels. This is interesting to note. We see Daniel, Jesus and others who have gone on a prolonged fast end up opening themselves up to angelic contact and ministering spirits. It seems that once the body is in an alkaline state that beings from higher realms of densities are able to approach us. In my personal encounters with the angelic realm, it was communicated to me that if I wished to continue encounters that I was to abstain from meat and give myself to prayer and meditation. The book of Clement gives a great deal of insight concerning how demons gain access to men who gorge themselves on meat.

"NOW THAT THE DEMONS ARE DESIROUS OF OCCUPYING THE BODIES OF MEN, THIS IS THE REASON. THEY ARE SPIRITS BARING THEIR PURPOSE TURNED TO WICKEDNESS. THEREFORE BY IMMODERATE EATING AND DRINKING, AND LUST, THEY URGE MEN ON TO SIN, BUT ONLY THOSE WHO ENTERTAIN THE PURPOSE OF SINNING, WHO, WHILE THEY SEEM SIMPLY DESIROUS OF SATISFYING THE NECESSARY CRAVINGS OF NATURE, GIVE OPPORTUNITY TO THE DEMONS TO ENTER INTO THEM, BECAUSE THROUGH EXCESS THEY DO NOT MAINTAIN MODERATION. | CHAPTER XVI

The text goes on to say that when excess meats are consumed, "gut rot" happens. Gut rot is when too much meat is consumed and it becomes stagnated within the belly. The meat turns bad before the body is able to process it. This is a major concern in the West because many people who suffer from obesity do not even know what it means to even be hungry. We are raised being taught that we are supposed to eat at certain times. We are supposed to have three square meals a day for breakfast, lunch, and dinner. We tend to eat when it is "time" to eat, before even feeling any pangs of hunger. Many westerners eat their next meal before their previous one is even digested. This leads to gut rot and has the body working overtime to try and break down these heavy meats and toxins.

Teratoma Tumors

Teratoma tumors are a rare type of tumor with less than 20,000 cases reported per year. Teratoma tumors are one of the most baffling phenomenon in medical science. These are tumors that contain other body parts growing inside of them. There are reports from the U.S. and China of children born having these tumors with feet, hands, teeth, hair and even eyes growing within them. Teratoma tumors are nothing new. Livescience reports that Spanish archaeologists found the remains of a 30 year old Roman woman who died 1,600 years ago with a calcified tumor in her pelvis. It had a bone and four deformed teeth embedded in it. The word teratoma comes from the Greek words "teras" and "onkoma" which translate to "monster" and "swelling," respectively. With all the study on demonology and how demons wish to influence their host, it is not out of the realm of possibility to suggest that these demons eventually wish to have bodies of their own. Could the Teratoma tumor possibly be the demonic spirit trying to form a body of its own in some strange way? It is also theorized that what many people call "grey aliens" are actually only suits that demons have animated and dwell within. Some suggest that these demonic entities have made pacts with our world leaders and that the government has created these dormant bodies for the demons to inhabit. I'm not too sure about that theory, but I have researched the Milab abductions (Military Abductions) and have found it quite frightening. Many people who claim to have been abducted aboard an alien spacecraft report being strapped down to tables with alien grey type beings running tests on them and extracting their DNA. The interesting thing is that many of these people report that they also see men in military garb on the ships watching these procedures take place. From my research I have found that the Milab projects were initiated to create fear and hysteria within Ufology. The powers that be do not want you making contact with the beings in the angelic realms.

Part 12
Fasting To Rid One's Self of Spirits

PART 13
OVERCOMING EVIL SPIRITS (JAMES 4:7)

Sometimes an evil spirit is sent out from God to teach someone a lesson. There are things that we must learn in the valley that cannot grow on the mountain top. In essence these evil spirits are servants of God carrying out his will. It is not fun while you are going through the storm, but this is the reason that God tells us over and over again throughout the scriptures to rejoice in our sufferings, trials and persecution. He actually says that it is a blessing when these things fall upon us. Why? Because it is producing something within us that cannot be imparted or learned unless we go through that particular struggle. In the midst of the struggle God has promised to protect us and we are still be able to maintain our peace, even when it looks like everything around us is falling apart. The first thing we do is begin to panic, much like Peter stepping out of the boat to be with Jesus. His childlike faith caused him to take the first step out of the boat and he began to walk on water just like Jesus. It wasn't until the reality of what was happening in the physical realm sunk in that he began to look at his situation and circumstance and take his eyes off of Jesus. Once this happened, fear entered his heart and he started to sink into the sea. There is a tangible peace that God promises us in the midst of the storm because Jesus is the one that has the power to speak to the winds and the waves. However, some of the spirits and demons that accompany the trial cannot be rebuked or cast out until we learn why they came in the first place. One of my favorite scriptures is James 4:7. I have personally found it to be a blueprint for navigating

Part 13
Overcoming Evil Spirits (James 4:7)

through the storms in ridding one's self from demonic attacks. In the church Christians blame the devil for everything, but we must remember that the devil only has the ability to do whatever God allows. God uses the devil to chastise and teach. James 4:7 reads,

SUBMIT YOURSELVES THEREFORE TO GOD. RESIST THE DEVIL, AND HE WILL FLEE FROM YOU. DRAW NIGH TO GOD, AND HE WILL DRAW NIGH TO YOU. CLEANSE YOUR HANDS, YE SINNERS; AND PURIFY YOUR HEARTS, YE DOUBLE MINDED. BE AFFLICTED, AND MOURN, AND WEEP: LET YOUR LAUGHTER BE TURNED TO MOURNING, AND YOUR JOY TO HEAVINESS. HUMBLE YOURSELVES IN THE SIGHT OF THE LORD, AND HE SHALL LIFT YOU UP.

This was actually one of the first scriptures that I ever learned and actually clung to coming out of witchcraft. I called in to a TBN prayer line and the person over the phone shared it with me and it has been near and dear to my heart ever since. Let's break down what I believe is a simple Biblical formula to ridding one's self of spirits and moving from glory to glory.

1. Submit yourselves therefore to God.

We must make sure that we are submitted to God in every area of our life. We must search our hearts to make sure that there is no hidden sin or wrong motive within us. If so that's ok, but we must deal with it. We must repent of the sin and ask God to forgive us. Sometimes this is easier said than done, but we must find the root of the issue. Are you judging someone? Participating in slander and accusations? Have you been hurt? Whatever it is we must seek the Lord for total healing so that these impure thoughts and desires no longer cling to us. We have to deal with them early on or will weigh us down and not allow us to ascend the hill of The Lord. Sometimes this can take years or months and other times it is demolished in a moment. This is why the scripture says,

"WHO SHALL ASCEND INTO THE HILL OF THE LORD? OR WHO SHALL STAND IN HIS HOLY PLACE? HE THAT HATH CLEAN HANDS, AND A PURE HEART; WHO HATH NOT LIFTED UP HIS SOUL UNTO VANITY, NOR SWORN DECEITFULLY. HE SHALL RECEIVE THE BLESSING FROM THE LORD, AND RIGHTEOUSNESS FROM THE GOD OF HIS SALVATION.| PSALM 24:3-5

The scriptures tell us time and time again that man judges by the outward appearance but God judges by the heart, motives and intentions. In order for the anointing to flow freely in our lives and to have open communication with the Holy Spirit, we must examine ourselves daily to make sure that we are in the faith. But be of good cheer, because this gets a little easier as we get used to this as a daily process. If we are submitted to God, we are protected by His mighty hand. When we go outside of His will we open ourselves up for demonic attack, but if we are submitted to Him in every area, then no matter what comes we know that it was allowed by Him for our good.

2. Resist the devil, and he will flee from you.

Resist the devil. Just show a little bit of resistance. Stop giving in to the temptation and falling over every stumbling block that is set before you. The scripture says that for every temptation we are faced with, God has provided us a way out. You have to show some resistance. After all, isn't this a spiritual battle? The battle is the Lord's and the warfare takes place in the span of twelve inches,

Part 13
Overcoming Evil Spirits (James 4:7)

the place between the heart and mind. It is also said that if we give the devil and inch twelve times, he becomes a ruler. This resistance is also a form of worship. Many people travail in prayer and beg God to take away temptations, drug addiction, pornography addiction etc., but it is in our denial of these momentarily fulfilling things that God gets the glory. Show some resistance. It is the only way that you will find freedom and be able to elevate to the greater levels that God is calling you to.

3. Draw nigh to God, and he will draw nigh to you.

It becomes easier to know when other spirits are trying to invade our heart space when we draw closer to God and the Holy Spirit. The more we get familiar with walking in the spirit and what that feels like, it becomes easier to tell when things are amiss. We can actually sense when other spirits are among us trying to settle in such as pride, lust and any evil imagination. This also naturally sharpens our gift of discernment because we know what the other spirits look and feel like, so we are able to stop them in their tracks early on. A lot of the trouble, stress and worry that believers find themselves in is uncalled for. Many times we make a mountain out of a molehill, and these trials could be over quickly if we just draw closer to the fire of God and let the impurities burn off in the refiner's fire. If it is God who allows these things to happen, it is He who is able to banish them. We are created with free will and we get to choose to worship God. Yes, sin is fun but for a season as the scripture says, but it is only God that can satisfy our souls. We always look for the quick fix, but in the end it is simply putting a band aid on an inner mortal wound. The Bible bids us to "choose this day who we will serve." Choosing God, the one who satisfies our soul over the pleasures of the flesh, is an act of worship. God gets the glory when we choose Him over the underwhelming competition. Our prayer should not be begging for forgiveness asking God to take these desires away, but to consciously choose God over these other things. Our desires will begin to shift if we continually do this and we will find that we have indeed created a mountain out of a molehill once we look back at the things the Lord has brought us out of.

I believe this is an easy check list that we can go through to examine ourselves and I believe that it will lead us to walk in victory in every area of our lives.

Part 13
Overcoming Evil Spirits (James 4:7)

PART 14
JESUS

Now that we've covered a wide and varying range of topics when it comes to the spirit world, what role does Jesus play in all of this? Who is Jesus and where does He fit in on the spectrum of all of these other spirits and entities? Engaging with some of these realms without the proper understanding of Christ and who He is can be detrimental. People have reported coming back demonically oppressed, possessed and have even gone mad while practicing some of these spiritual practices without the proper context. Knowing who Christ is and who you are in him makes all the difference. Jesus is the first born of all creation and everything that was created was created through Him and for Him.

"For by Him all things were created, in the heavens and on the earth, things visible and things invisible, whether thrones or dominions or principalities or powers; all things have been created through Him, and for Him. He is before all things, and in Him all things are held together" (Col. 1:16,17).

What does it mean to have the authority of Christ? Every knee must bow and every tongue must confess that Jesus Christ is Lord. That goes for all the spirits in the ethers, elementals, demons, angels and all others. They ALL must submit to the authority of Jesus Christ. Jesus is the most beautiful thing that you can encounter, for He is universal love of God made manifest into a being. He is the Word of God that became flesh and dwelt among men. He is the embodiment of love that became a person.

Part 14
Jesus

Divine Mercy (by Eugeniusz Kazimirowski in 1934

There is so much to encounter in the etheric and heavenly realms, but I believe that Jesus takes the cake every time. Every encounter is a new realm of who He is and that will never get old. His beauty and splendor is comparable to none! He is the alpha and omega, the first and the last, the beginning and the end, He is everything. His only intention is love. Love for you, me and everyone in humanity. No matter what happens, perfect love is always the driving force of Christ. There is a peace that dwells within the believer who knows who they are in Christ. There is also a freedom that accompanies us as we explore the other realms without fear and with perfect peace. There are all types of misconceptions and half-truths about some of the taboo spiritual practices that the church forbids, such as meditation and yoga. There are people who teach that if you empty out your mind and get quiet, demons will enter into the quiet places of the mind leading to demonic possession. This is so far from the truth. This teaching has led to many people becoming overly busy and absent from the stillness of the presence of God. There is nothing to fear as long as your motives and intentions are pure. Many are called but the chosen are few. Lots of times, people stay in the outer courts of the supernatural things of God for fear of getting possessed by the devil or demons, which causes them to miss what God is doing in the Earth today. We MUST use proper precautions in engaging in other spiritual realms, but the spirit of Christ beckons his followers into a mystical journey of exploration. Jesus is the gate and the way that we enter in. The Father has so much to show us if we would only come. The basis for the majority of my work is to show people that many things that have been deemed "new age" or "demonic" are in fact scriptural and were practiced by the prophets and disciples throughout the Bible. We have given our spirituality away to other religions and belief systems and thus have forfeited our birthright, but thanks be to God that there is a revival and renewal of the ancient ways. Every spiritual encounter is a new way to experience God, a new way to communicate and receive the fullness of what the Father has for us. No one way is better than the other, but all are needed and all work together cohesively for the believer to operate in the spirit realm and walk in freedom and authority in the Earth.

The Light of Christ

One night while seeking the Lord in prayer with two friends of mine, Matt and Shane, I received a life-changing vision of Jesus. We were in Matt's living room holding hands in prayer and asking God for a visitation. About two hours into our prayer , something happened. With my eyes closed I began to see a figure walking towards me in the spirit realm. As the figure got closer I knew it was Jesus. I could not make out any details of his face. All I could see was his silhouette, but his presence was so familiar. The silhouette was a being made of a white light with a bright yellow glow. As Jesus approached me, his aura began to get brighter and brighter and with each step I felt more and more of his love until suddenly I was overtaken. Then my eyes clasp shut even tighter and the beautiful radiating white light over took my vision until it was all that I saw. The euphoria was so overwhelming, unlike anything that I had ever experienced. It felt so good to feel God's love on my body reaching all the way down to my inner being. His love wasn't the only thing that I felt. I could feel his burden and brokenness toward humanity. His love was coupled with a great sorrow that, while euphoric and beautiful, also felt gut-wrenching and painful. The pain was so intense that I could not stop myself from screaming out at the top of my lungs. While still holding their hands my body slammed backwards to the ground. My whole body was vibrating and Matt and Shane could also feel the energy pulsating through me. They said that the energy was so beautiful that they didn't want to let go of my hands for fear that they wouldn't be able to feel it anymore. Matt was a little afraid that the neighbors might call the cops because I was screaming so loudly.

I've had many amazing encounters in the presence of God, but this one left me changed. I walked away from that night with an impartation and a different perspective. I received a deeper burden for the world and got to feel God's compassion towards all of humanity.

Part 14
Jesus

PART 15
SPIRITUAL GIFTINGS AND PSYCHIC ABILITIES

Words are more powerful than we could ever imagine. There are some keys to keep in mind when moving under the spirit of prophecy. 1 Corinthians 14:3 says "But the one who prophesies speaks to people for their strengthening, encouraging and comfort." Although some words that come through can seem harsh, everything should be filtered through the lens of love. God's heart is always for restoration. Many times we miss the mark or get off the path and it is His love that draws us back to him.

1 CORINTHIANS 14:24 LETS US KNOW THE REASONING BEHIND THE USE OF THE PROPHETIC UTTERANCE "BUT IF AN UNBELIEVER OR AN INQUIRER COMES IN WHILE EVERYONE IS PROPHESYING, THEY ARE CONVICTED OF SIN AND ARE BROUGHT UNDER JUDGMENT BY ALL, AS THE SECRETS OF THEIR HEARTS ARE LAID BARE. SO THEY WILL FALL DOWN AND WORSHIP GOD, EXCLAIMING, "GOD IS REALLY AMONG YOU!"

The chapter goes on the say that we may ALL prophesy and encourages us to be eager to do so.

God has given each one of his children spiritual giftings and abilities that we are able to use to bring healing to the nations and make his name known in the Earth. Each of these specific gifts is for us to share his heart with the world. These gifts and abilities were used as tools in the Bible to communicate the gospel to people and act as signs

Part 15
Spiritual Giftings and Psychic Abilities

and wonders. These gifts were used to let people know that God had not forgotten about them. The prophetic giftings let people know that God knows their past, present and future. At times God will share information with the believer to convey these messages. The more we use them the better we get at being able to sense the way that God is speaking. We have physical senses and those senses are mirrored in the spirit and we are able to see, hear and feel impressions from the other realms. These are tools that one can use for good or bad. There is a variety of beings that are trying to communicate with us from the other side. Just as we are able to use the tools to connect with our Heavenly Father and beings within the angelic orders, we are also subjected to lower spirits according to the vibrational density that one is walking in. If you choose the wide path of drunkenness, debauchery, lying and deceiving you will attract the same type of beings that are tied to those behaviors. If you choose the narrow path of love, light and forgiveness you will likewise entertain the beings upon that level of density as well.

NOW THERE ARE DIVERSITIES OF GIFTS, BUT THE SAME SPIRIT. AND THERE ARE DIFFERENCES OF ADMINISTRATIONS, BUT THE SAME LORD. AND THERE ARE DIVERSITIES OF OPERATIONS, BUT IT IS THE SAME GOD WHICH WORKETH ALL IN ALL. BUT THE MANIFESTATION OF THE SPIRIT IS GIVEN TO EVERY MAN TO PROFIT WITHAL. FOR TO ONE IS GIVEN BY THE SPIRIT THE WORD OF WISDOM; TO ANOTHER THE WORD OF KNOWLEDGE BY THE SAME SPIRIT; TO ANOTHER FAITH BY THE SAME SPIRIT; TO ANOTHER THE GIFTS OF HEALING BY THE SAME SPIRIT; TO ANOTHER THE WORKING OF MIRACLES; TO ANOTHER PROPHECY; TO ANOTHER DISCERNING OF SPIRITS; TO ANOTHER DIVERS KINDS OF TONGUES; TO ANOTHER THE INTERPRETATION OF TONGUES: BUT ALL THESE WORKETH THAT ONE AND THE SELFSAME SPIRIT, DIVIDING TO EVERY MAN SEVERALLY AS HE WILL. | 1 CORINTHIANS 12:4-11

Spirit Realm: Angels, Demons, Spirits and the Sovereignty of God

All through the Bible we read about normal people doing the miraculous. We read about them interacting with angels, spirits and ghosts by the way of hearing voices, seeing prophetic visions in the dream and waking states, etc. We also read about them performing mighty miracles to accomplish the will of God on the Earth and to give glory back to the Father. Everyone from the Old Testament prophets and seers to the New Testament disciples, apostles and even Jesus operated in spiritual giftings and supernatural encounters were very much at work in their lives. When studying the gifts of the spirit mentioned in 1 Conrinthians 12, it helps to look into the psychic abilities and ESP (Extra Sensory Perception) practiced in many spiritual circles.

Many in Christendom get scared when we mention terms and phrases like ESP or Clairvoyance, Clairaudience, Claircognizance and Clairsentience. It might be because these terms aren't actually in the Bible by these names, but many Christian leaders within the prophetic ministry are teaching these techniques with a Biblical approach. The Bible is full of mysticism and ecstatic encounters with Jesus, ghosts, angels and divine beings and for Christians to deny this aspect of their faith is denying a part of the Godhead itself. Every faith likes to pretend that they own exclusivity to spiritual terms and ideas. They like to claim that their approach is the only way that things can be done, yet this is not the case at all. Syncretism allows us to look at all religions and ideas and be able to see the similarities within the very fabric of the faiths. Doing this allows us to see that we are not so different after all. Spiritual gifts and psychic abilities is the perfect concept to bring to this discussion, especially when we see Jesus and the disciples practicing the techniques listed above. They didn't use the same terms in the Bible today so the wording is a bit different. The Bible uses terms like prophesy, word of wisdom, word of knowledge and quickening to name a few. The Bible even talks about

Part 15
Spiritual Giftings and Psychic Abilities

going into trances and receiving visions from the spirit world. It also talks about out of body experiences and astral projection but uses terms like rapture or "being caught up". The apostle Paul even shares about an experience where he traveled to heaven. He states that the experience was so beautiful and real that he did not know if he went there in the spirit as in "leaving his body" or if he was "translated" with his body and all. There are even more similarities between Christianity and what is deemed New Age than commonly thought.

Jesus went out performing many miracles and making decisions based upon following the flow or unction of the Holy Spirit, which spoke to him in many different ways. God uses the miraculous as an open door to share His love with mankind. There are many examples in the scripture where Jesus used his spiritual giftings as an open door as well. The miracles and supernatural encounters act as a bridge and at times reveal the inner secrets of the heart that only God knows.

Spirit Realm: Angels, Demons, Spirits and the Sovereignty of God

The Woman at the Well

Carl Heinrich Bloch - Woman at the Well Carl Heinrich Bloch

In the story of the woman at the well in John chapter 4, Jesus meets a woman fetching water from a well. In conversation with her, he uses the water as an analogy about being spiritually dry and the water that he provides causes us to never thirst again. In their discourse Jesus tells her out of the blue to "GO, CALL YOUR HUSBAND AND COME BACK" and she replies that she has no husband. Jesus, operating under the word of knowledge, says cynically "YOU ARE RIGHT WHEN YOU SAY THAT YOU HAVE 'NO HUSBAND' FOR IN FACT YOU HAVE HAD FIVE HUSBANDS AND THE MAN THAT YOU ARE WITH NOW IS NOT YOUR HUSBAND." Jesus had no foreknowledge of her situation according to the flesh. He was just passing through the city, but God had bestowed upon him a divine appointment. The woman then says "SIR, I CAN SEE THAT YOU ARE A PROPHET", acknowledging his gift. Jesus then begins to share the truth of the gospel with her and tells her that he is the messiah. As the woman leaves and returns to town, she begins to tell people "COME AND SEE A MAN WHO HAS TOLD ME EVERYTHING THAT I HAVE EVER DONE; COULD THIS BE THE MESSIAH?" After this, the town's

Part 15
Spiritual Giftings and Psychic Abilities

people began to make their way towards Jesus. Verse 39 says that many of the Samaritans from that town believed on him because of that woman's testimony and they urged him to stay with them, and he did for two days. During the two days that Jesus was with them, the people told the woman **"We no longer believe just because of what you said; now we have heard for ourselves, and we know that this man really is the Savior of the world."** One supernatural word of knowledge caused many people to come to faith in God because of Jesus's willingness and obedience to be used by the Father. This is why Jesus later goes on to say "Unless you people see signs and wonders, you will never believe." This is but one example of how God uses spiritual giftings and abilities to win people over and draw them unto himself. How does God do this? Through us.

Ephesians 2:10 says, **For we are Gods workmanship, created in Christ Jesus unto good works, which God prepared in advance for us to do.**

This is the song and dance with God, the divine romance; that God would use us to bring forth His glory upon the Earth. Jesus and the disciples were privy to these spiritual giftings and abilities, and Jesus also left a promise that we would do greater things than him!

Everyone has the ability to tap into these spiritual functions for themselves. They are what we call the sixth sense. Have you ever thought about someone and then they suddenly called you on the phone? Have you ever thought about an old song that you haven't heard in years and then the radio Dj randomly played it as you thought of it? These are minor examples of how we are tuned into our spiritual senses and psychic abilities. The amazing thing is that you can actually hone in on them and get better at using them just like a muscle gets stronger the more you use it. The more aware we are of the presence of these in our life, the more we can open ourselves up for these "God Encounters". We have learned to better hear God's voice while in prayer by using the laying on of hands during group gatherings. It's about being able to be quiet and tap into the person's energy. By doing this we can sense, feel and know what they are going through and we can minister directly to their specific need. Instead of praying a hundred words that just seem to end in monotony, we can learn to pray and speak 10 words of power. God cares about all of us. He cares about every aspect and every area of our lives, and He even knows what we need before we pray. Each one of us can learn to be so close to the heart of the Father that we not only know His heart and desire for our own lives, but also the lives and purposes of those around us.

When we think of terms like psychic abilities and sixth sense our mind goes to new age and paganism, but the interesting thing is that these types of spiritual giftings are also mentioned in the Bible. Jesus and his disciples used these spiritual powers and the anointing to bring forth healing and deliverance to many during their ministry. It has been said that to deny these spiritual gifts and talents is to deny people an aspect of Jesus. If Jesus and His disciples needed these tools during their ministry, then how much more do we?

Part 15
Spiritual Giftings and Psychic Abilities

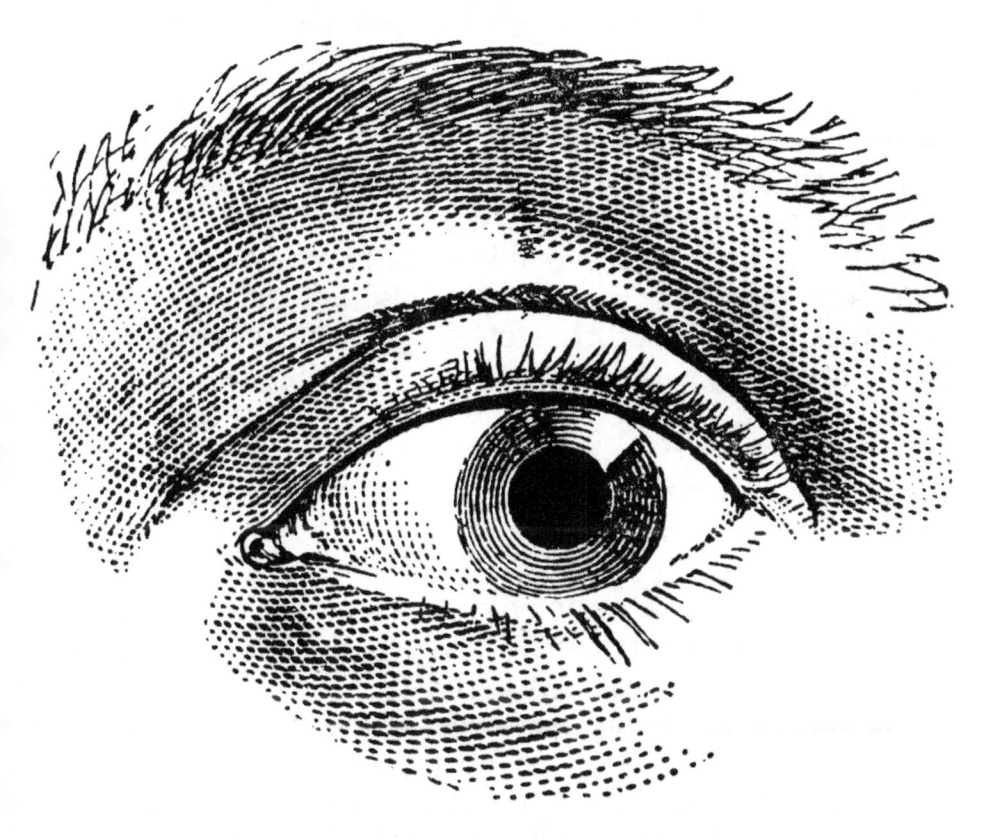

Clairvoyance (Clear Seeing)

"AND IT SHALL COME TO PASS AFTERWARD, THAT I WILL POUR OUT MY SPIRIT ON ALL FLESH; YOUR SONS AND YOUR DAUGHTERS SHALL PROPHESY, YOUR OLD MEN SHALL DREAM DREAMS, AND YOUR YOUNG MEN SHALL SEE VISIONS." | JOEL 2:28

There are many different ways of seeing in the spirit. Some people are able to see auras around a person, some claim to see angels or demons around when others cannot and some immediately see prophetic images from heaven when they close their eyes. I have personally been in meetings and during prayer have been able to see snakes on people or chains wrapped around their feet symbolizing demonic strongholds and forces working against the person. I immediately began to intercede for the person and by faith reach down and undo the chains. When faith meets action it brings about change. Often the person would feel a heaviness lift off of them and feel an immediate wave of God's presence when something like this occurred. Sometimes God requires us to step out in faith in order to see the miraculous. We must step out from our comfort zone, which is an act of denying ourselves. The scripture states that obedience is better than sacrifice. Once God opens the eye of our understanding we begin to walk in a greater level of consciousness and believe God for more. This is a realm where the supernatural becomes natural and it becomes a part of our daily life.

In 2 Kings 6, Elisha went on a journey with a young man when they ran into trouble. They woke up in the morning surrounded by a great army and fear immediately struck the heart of the young man. Elisha then turns to him and says "DON'T BE AFRAID. THOSE WHO ARE WITH US ARE MORE THAN THOSE WHO ARE WITH THEM." AND ELISHA PRAYED, "OPEN HIS EYES, LORD, SO THAT HE MAY SEE." THEN THE LORD OPENED THE SERVANT'S EYES, AND HE LOOKED AND SAW THE HILLS FULL OF HORSES AND CHARIOTS OF FIRE ALL AROUND ELISHA.

Elisha's prayer opened up the young man's eyes to be able to see the spiritual reality of what was really going on. If God is for us then there are none that can stand against us. We are in a spiritual battle and we have armies of angelic hosts surrounding us. Sometimes we are able to see them in the spirit and it builds our faith. Ask God to allow you to see in the spirit. Ask the Father to open your eyes, but be careful, what you see may shock you.

Faith is being able to see a thing manifested before it is physically here. When we prophesy over our lives or the lives of others, we must have a picture in our minds of the outcome that we wish to see. Then we step out by faith, proclaim it and by doing so, birth it into reality. Faith equipped with vision and expectancy is what brings about miracles.

Clairscent (Clear Smelling)

Clairscent, also known as Clairolfaction, is a form of extra-sensory perception that enables a person to receive psychic or paranormal information by means of 'psychic smelling'. Some people are able to smell energies or intent as a way of spiritual discernment. It is believed by some that when you smell a fragrance that reminds you of a loved one that has passed on that they are trying to communicate or say hello. For example, a person may smell their grandfather's favorite cologne or smell mothballs, a scent that immediately takes them back to grandma's house when they were children. Smelling is also synonymous with inner knowing i.e. "I smell something fishy going on here".

Often a foul or demonic spirit carries with it a rude stench similar to that of garbage, vomit or rotting flesh. Many people have experienced this smell while performing exorcisms during the deliverance of demonic spirits. On the other hand while in ecstatic experiences with God, there are accounts of smelling beautiful aromas of honey, incense, frankincense, flowers and sweet smelling fragrances. Song of Solomon 1:3 says, "PLEASING IS THE FRAGRANCE OF YOUR PERFUMES; YOUR NAME IS LIKE PERFUME POURED OUT". The Bible refers back to our prayers, deeds and alms rising up to heaven as a fragrance before the Lord. The priest also burned incense during times of prayer believing that the smoke would carry their prayers to heaven as an offering before God.

Clairaudience (Clear Hearing)

God is always speaking. The question is, are we listening? In 1 Samuel Chapter 3, Samuel hears a voice calling out to him in the middle of the night. Samuel hears the voice and gets up on three occasions thinking that it was the High Priest Eli that was calling his name. On the third occasion, Eli tells Samuel, "It is not me calling you, maybe it is the Lord. The next time you hear your name called say, 'Speak Lord, for your servant is listening'". When he did this the next time God began to speak with Samuel. Sometimes we can hear His voice deep within our being, sometimes as audibly as speaking with a friend. Learning the different ways that God is speaking is a beautiful journey.

2 Chronicles 16:9 says, "The eyes of the Lord search the whole earth in order to strengthen those whose hearts are fully committed to him." God is always speaking and always looking for those who are willing to draw near and hear what He has to say. One of the most powerful and wisest experiences that I have come to practice (whether in corporate prayer for someone else or in my personal quiet time) is to just sit in silence and ask the Father, "Lord, What would you say? We know what men would say and what they have said, I know what I would say, but Lord, what would you say?" The first thing that we should do in every situation is consult the heart of the Father and ask for His guidance in the matter. I guarantee you that every time He will speak. It may not be through a sign or wonder. We may not audibly hear his voice but if we pay attention, he is speaking.

Jesus said in John 10 "My sheep hear my voice." This means that those whom he has called are able to both literally and figuratively "hear" his voice in various ways.

Part 15
Spiritual Giftings and Psychic Abilities

God speaks to our hearts through his still small voice. He speaks through His written word and many other ways mentioned in this segment on ESP. Learning to distinguish the voice of the Father comes through levels of discernment. The Bible is a great plumb line and God will never speak anything contrary to His word. In the charismatic movement many people come daily with revelations saying that God told them this or God told them that when in fact God hasn't spoken to them in years. I've heard scenarios where people have said God told them to leave their wife, God told them it was ok to smoke meth, God told them it was okay to look at porn and many other crazy things that not only go outside of His word but against it. We need to be wary of new revelations and always test it against Gods word. In fact it is quite easy to get off track and follow a stranger's voice. In many cases the stranger's voice may even be our own. We have two primary voices being heard, the will of God and our own. These two desires are constantly wrestling with one another. Just as Jacob wrestled with God and was left changed, we too wrestle with Him in the ring of our mind. Sometimes people want to believe things so badly that they put words in Gods mouth and then begin to tell people, "HERE IS WHAT GOD TOLD ME".
The scripture says in Psalm 37:4-5:

DELIGHT THYSELF ALSO IN THE LORD: AND HE SHALL GIVE THEE THE DESIRES OF THINE HEART. COMMIT THY WAY UNTO THE LORD; TRUST ALSO IN HIM; AND HE SHALL BRING IT TO PASS.

If we delight ourselves in The Lord, He will give us the desires of our hearts. The key is that when we delight ourselves in God, our desires begin to change. Through the sanctification process and the renewing of the mind we will eventually no longer desire the same things that we used to. For example, when we used to desire to sin, acquire material possessions or to be famous, our joy was in those things, not fully in the Lord. Through spending time delighting ourselves in the Lord, we may now desire righteousness and to live Holy and be content.

Claircognizance (Clear Knowing)

AND, BEHOLD, CERTAIN OF THE SCRIBES SAID WITHIN THEMSELVES, THIS MAN BLASPHEMETH. AND JESUS KNOWING THEIR THOUGHTS SAID, WHEREFORE THINK YE EVIL IN YOUR HEARTS? | MATTHEW 9:3-4

Claircognizance in the Bible is called a "Word of Knowledge" or "Word of Wisdom". The Holy Spirit will speak to you about things that you need to know or inform you how to make a decision. These are usually things that you would have no way of knowing unless given direct knowledge from God. You may know a person's name, where they work or some significant detail about them that you had no other way of knowing. This is also referred to as a quickening or divine revelation in the scriptures. Many Christian circles are starting to use the term "download" as well. This gifting also correlates with the discernment of spirits. We are able to know things about people without even meeting them before. When a person is oppressed with a spirit or may have a particular familiar spirit around them, those who have the gift of discernment are able to discern which spirit is upon that person as well.

The Word of Wisdom is divine revelation on how to use or share knowledge. Just because it's a divine revelation does not mean that we are to go out and share it with everyone. Jesus warns us in Matthew 7:6 not to cast our pearls before swine because they will trample them under their feet. In a world where many still feel the need to be affirmed, often we are very eager to run and share our new revelation with friends or leadership. One of the biggest crushing blows that a believer can experience is sharing their revelation with someone and they think that you are way off or not hearing from God. There is a saying that those who live for the approval of others will die by their rejection. A way to avoid this is by the use of wisdom. If God spoke it, it will remain. He will confirm it by His presence and with signs and wonders and the impact will bear much fruit. It will be something that lasts versus just some idea that came and went. This principal is shown to us in the story of Joseph and the coat of many colors. Joseph was given a vision of what he was to do in the future, and it was something great. So great that even his older brother would be subservient under him. When he shared this dream with them, they were immediately offended and plotted within their hearts to put him away and harm him. They were jealous and insecure within their own callings and identities. Like us, Joseph may have shared his vision with the world prematurely, but God has a beautiful way of working every situation out for our good.

Grieving The Holy Spirit

I remember one of the first times I knew deep in my spirit that I was supposed to do something that God was asking me to do. The Lord spoke deep down in my spirit on an occasion while my wife, a friend and I were in the checkout line at Walmart. We didn't have much money at the time, and only had enough to buy the few things that we needed and still grab some fast food burgers on the way home. While we were in line, as soon as I laid eye on the lady ahead of us, The Lord spoke to me and specifically told me to pay for her groceries. My carnal mind immediately set in and I started trying to rationalize the notion. I began to try and explain it away as "Well, maybe that's the devil speaking to me so I won't have money to eat" and "I'm not sure if I'll have enough money to buy her things and ours too". All of these weird doubts immediately crept in but the voice of the Lord continued to speak even stronger. "Pay for her groceries", yet I continued to try and quiet the inner voice of God knowing that I was telling God no due to my own fear or selfishness. As the woman proceeded to have her groceries rung up, the cashier told her the cost and the woman said, "Oh, well I'll have to put a few things back". The woman grabbed two or three items and set them to the side, paid for her remaining items and left. This whole time I feel the voice of the Holy Spirit screaming to my spirit "Pay for her groceries," yet I still didn't. The lady grabbed her bag and walked out of the store. At closer inspection, the lady only had three can goods and a banana. The feeling that came over me was like no other. I had felt for the first time what it feels like to grieve the Holy Spirit. I felt like someone punched me in the stomach. We beg and beg God to use us. We fast and study for divine revelation to share with others, yet we miss Him on the small things. I learned a huge lesson that day. Do not grieve the Holy Spirit. I felt as if I gave God the cold shoulder on such a small opportunity for God to use me. From that moment on, I told the Lord if He would forgive me and continue to speak that I would never let it happen again. The Lord showed mercy and put me in many other similar situations where I was able to see the hand of God move through my small acts of faith. Obedience is better than sacrifice, and God is a rewarder to those that genuinely seek Him. If God can trust you with the small things He will make you ruler over more. If God can't trust me with a $3 Walmart purchase, then He can't trust me with a $300 light bill for someone else.

HIS LORD SAID TO HIM, 'WELL DONE, GOOD AND FAITHFUL SERVANT; YOU HAVE BEEN FAITHFUL OVER A FEW THINGS, I

Part 15
Spiritual Giftings and Psychic Abilities

WILL MAKE YOU RULER OVER MANY THINGS. ENTER INTO THE JOY OF YOUR LORD.' | MATTHEW 25:21

Clairsentience (Clear Feeling)

In Mark Chapter 5, we read the story of the woman with the issue of blood and how by her faith she was made whole. An interesting thing about this story is when the woman touched Jesus that He "felt" the virtue or power leave him. The feeling was so strong that He turned around in a crowded street with people all around to ask, "WHO TOUCHED ME?" This is one example about feeling the presence of God, power or anointing physically.

There are several references in the New Testament about how Jesus was moved with compassion for those who were lost or sick. Jesus bore a natural empathy for those people and believers also continued to carry this burden for a lost and dying world.

SEEING THEN THAT WE HAVE A GREAT HIGH PRIEST, THAT IS PASSED INTO THE HEAVENS, JESUS THE SON OF GOD, LET US HOLD FAST OUR PROFESSION. FOR WE HAVE NOT AN HIGH PRIEST WHICH CANNOT BE TOUCHED WITH THE FEELING OF OUR INFIRMITIES | HEBREWS 4:14-15

Just as Hebrews says that Jesus is moved by our infirmities, we carry the very same nature to the world by unction of the Holy Spirit. We carry a compassion that we can at many times feel within the depths of our beings. There are times of travail when the Holy Spirit will pray for us with groanings and utterances not understood by human intellect. Many times when this occurs you are able to feel what area you are receiving healing in. This also happens in times of deep intercession with others. There is a feeling associated with the prayers.

Many people speak about being empathic and being able to pick up on other people's energy and feel it in their bodies. People who identify as empathic speak about not wanting to go out in public or visit Walmart because of all of the different energies that they will pick up on. I remember years ago showing up for pre-service prayer before youth service. We would sometimes show up an hour early in a separate room to prepare our hearts, ask God to move in power and pray for the people coming to encounter His love. On one particular evening, we walked into the dimly lit room with worship music playing and as soon as I stepped through the threshold of the doorway I felt this overwhelmingly strong burden of heaviness come upon me. I remember being in a pretty good mood and then instantly I felt overwhelmed and hopeless. As we walked into the room we were surprised to find another one of the church members over in the corner crying. We asked her if anything was wrong and she told us that she had just found out that her husband had been having an affair. Her heart was broken and the Lord allowed us to feel her burden supernaturally so that we would be moved with compassion and so we would minister healing to her.

Many times when we get these sensations, it is something that hits us spiritually and other times we can literally feel it in our bodies as a spirit of infirmity. When I first started having bodily pains in this way, I admit that the first thought I had was fear. It wasn't until I began to step out and exercise faith or ask God about the feeling that I started to see breakthroughs happen in people's lives. Once we were in a home meeting with a small group. During worship, I caught an excruciating pain in my neck. The first thing that came to my mind was fear, thinking that I pulled something. I immediately began to rebuke

Part 15
Spiritual Giftings and Psychic Abilities

the devil under my breath and command him to let my neck go, but nothing happened. "Devil, I am the healed of the Lord and no harm shall come nigh my dwelling, loose my neck in Jesus' name." Still nothing. I then paused for a second and thought about it and said to myself, "What if the Lord is allowing me to feel someone else's pain and this pain isn't even my own?" Again fear came, because now I've got to speak up in front of everyone and what if I was wrong? Thoughts continued to creep in, like, "People may think you don't hear God." Well, I'll never find out if I never try. After all, I had vowed to not grieve the Holy Spirit again. I didn't want someone to miss out on their healing because I was too shy. So I stood up and asked the room if anyone was having neck pain, and when I did a friend said, "Yes, I actually went to the doctor today because of my neck." By faith I said "Well, I believe that the Lord wants to heal you. Can we pray for you?" He said yes. We stood up and laid hands on him and the Spirit of God showed up, moved upon him and he said that the pain left! This began to happen to me more in other gatherings as well as at the doctor's office. For some reason fear usually likes rear its ugly head and try to get you to doubt God, but once you move past fear and into faith you will see the miraculous happen.

I was in a church service once during worship and I was having a beautiful time in the presence of God, when suddenly I went deaf in my right ear. Fear showed up and I began to ponder why this was happening. Maybe my blood pressure is off… or… maybe the Lord wants to open a deaf ear! I then got excited and stepped to the side to ask the pastor, who was a friend of mine if I could speak after the song was over. I told him the situation and he said yes. I went up to the stage and called it out. "Is there anyone here who is deaf in their right ear?" I looked around the room and an elderly gentleman stood up. I asked him to come to the front. I laid my hands upon him and commanded his ear to be open and the man was healed!

I can give many more examples where this continued happening again and again. I cannot stress enough that almost every time it did, fear showed up first. God uses our imagination, not our intellect. Make sure that your mind is renewed and you know who you are in Christ so that you will remain a pure vessel for the Lord to use. His heart will move to you and through you and perfect love casts out all fear!

Part 15
Spiritual Giftings and Psychic Abilities

PART 16
LIST OF SPIRITS MENTIONED AND THEIR FUNCTIONS

Spirit of Adoption
Rom 8:15
"the *placing* as a *son*, that is, *adoption* (figuratively Christian *sonship* in respect to God)"

The Spirit of Adoption has to be understood through sonship and understanding how the father and son relationship works within the covenant of God. The scriptures call the individuals who go about doing wickedness "the children of the devil" and those whose hearts are after righteousness "the children of God". Spiritual adoption takes place when God draws us to Himself, takes away our heart of stone and gives us a heart of flesh. Once this happens, our hearts that once desired to do wickedness now cry out Abba Father. Through this adoption, the Holy Spirit seals our hearts through faith in Christ. Although we may still stumble, we continue to get back up. The scriptures declare for though the righteous fall seven times, they rise again, but the wicked stumble when calamity strikes in Proverbs 24:16. This is also shown in the story of the prodigal son.

Part 16
List of Spirits Mentioned and Their Functions

Spirit of fear; Power, Love, Sound Mind
2Timothy 1:7
"(to *be* put in *fear*); *alarm* or *fright:* - be afraid"

Fear

The spirit of fear uses intimidation to cause one to worry, doubt and live in unbelief. Fear is in direct opposition to faith and can hinder the flow of confidence that it takes to walk in the spirit of Christ. This spirit causes its host to play out scenarios that do not or may never exist, making one afraid and hopeless. It is said that the acronym for the word FEAR is False Evidence Appearing Real, and this makes perfect sense.

When discussing the spirit of fear we must also address the healthy types of fear mentioned in the scriptures, such as the fear of The Lord. The Bible says this fear is the beginning of wisdom. This fear is more of a respect for His authority rather than being afraid of Him. Proverbs 8:13 says that The fear of the LORD *is* to hate evil: pride, and arrogancy, and the evil way. This is wisdom.

Power
"Greek word 'Dunamis' which means miracle working power/ Might, Strength"

Power relates back to Acts chapter 1:8, "But ye shall receive power, after that the Holy Ghost is come upon you: and ye shall be witnesses unto me both in Jerusalem, and in all Judaea, and in Samaria, and unto the uttermost part of the earth."

Through the anointing of the Holy Spirit, we receive power to be witnesses unto God. That's the "dunamis", or the miracle working power. The scripture also says in Mark 16:17, "And these signs shall follow them that believe; In my name shall they cast out devils; they shall speak with new tongues." Throughout the scriptures we see the prophets, disciples and apostles doing supernatural feats including healing, divine multiplication, prophesying, foretelling the future and having knowledge of the past, casting out of demons and performing many other great signs and wonders. This power was not just for them, but their exploits are left as an example for us. The writings of Paul urge believers to desire and to "lust" after spiritual gifts that are freely given by God to all.

Love

2 Timothy speaks about the Spirit of Love. In scripture, the Greek word used and its context is very important, because there are different words for love that show varying degrees of how much love is being shown. The Greek word used here for love is Agape, which is the greatest form of love and is also one of the manifested fruits of The Holy Spirit. It is no respecter of persons and knows no wrongs. The other types of love mentioned in the New Testament are from the words Phileo, Storge and Eros.

Phileo is the love we have towards friends and it oftentimes can we wavered and built upon stipulations.
Storge love is the love that parents instinctually have towards their children and shows a deeper connection in friendship that the Phileo type of love.
Eros is the passionate and romantic type of love dealing with the emotions and on a sexual level.

Part 16
List of Spirits Mentioned and Their Functions

These three levels of love can change in a person's life and relationship due to circumstance and actions, but the Agape form of love is the highest of the named words for love. This is the love that the Heavenly Father extends towards us, and we are to take that same love into the world through fellowship with The Holy Spirit. Some of the traits of this love can be found in the book of Galatians chapter 5:22-23, which reads, "But the fruit of the Spirit is love, joy, peace, patience, kindness, goodness, faithfulness, gentleness, and self-control." These are the manifested character traits that come from The Spirit of Love. These are specifications by which Jesus commands us to judge all things. We are not to judge by doctrine or dogma, but by their fruit. Out of all things, Love is the greatest.

A Sound Mind

The spirit of a sound mind is like the previous example of Agape love, because its essence comes out of fellowship with God through spiritual practice. It is also mentioned as a fruit of the Holy Spirit. The meaning comes from the Greek word meaning temperance or self-control. When studying these principles, in order for one thing to be true, the exact opposite must also apply. The opposite of self-control is what the scriptures call having "Fits of Rage". These are known as the deeds of the flesh. The spirit of a sound mind is in operation when the world is falling apart all around us, but we are able to keep cool, calm and collected in these situations. This is a peace that is supernatural because it comes straight from Jesus as mentioned in John 14:27, "Peace I leave with you, my peace I give unto you: not as the world giveth, give I unto you. Let not your heart be troubled, neither let it be afraid. It is what we call a peace that surpasses all understanding."

Deaf, Dumb & Foul Spirit
Mark 9:25

The deaf and dumb spirit is a literal spirit of infirmity that causes one to not be able to hear or speak. These spirits can be cast out by the power of God and the anointing of the Holy Spirit. The Testament of Solomon says of these spirits in verse 54, *"But I blind children in women's wombs, and twirl their ears round. And I make them deaf and mute. And I have again in my third head means of slipping in. And I smite men in the limbless part of the body, and cause them to fall down, and foam, and grind their teeth. But I have my own way of being frustrated, Jerusalem being signified in writing, unto the place called 'of the head." For there is fore-appointed the angel of the great counsel, and now he will openly dwell on the cross. He doth frustrate me, and to him am I subject."*

The deaf spirit is mentioned in the Testament of Solomon in verse 76, "The fifth (demon) said: "I am called Iudal, and I bring about a block in the ears and deafness of hearing. If I hear, 'Uruel Iudal,' I at once retreat."

The Testament of Solomon is a key piece of writing in understanding how spirits work and operate. It also gives info on which demonic spirits are associated with different ailments and infirmities, and also includes the accompanying angels and planets that bind them.

These spirits work by intimidation, causing people to be void of understanding and knowledge and causing them not to be able to learn or hear the truth.

These spirits can cause someone who knows the truth to be intimidated into keeping silent, succumbing to self-doubt, fear, and timidity. The spirits understand the power of the spoken word in confessions (1Jn 1:9), positive affirmations (Pro 18:21) and declarations (Rom 10:9-10). These spirits know about the law of binding and losing. They would stop at nothing for you to be blind to the power that resides within you.

Foul Spirit

"*impure* (ceremonially, morally (*lewd*) or specifically (*demonic*)): - foul, unclean."

The foul spirit abides on its hosts and entices one to be lewd and nasty in manner and language. There are times during the deliverance of this demon that the person undergoes a change of countenance. Their face could change, even morphing on some occasions. I have seen some of the most shy and polite people change in an instant and begin to utter the most horrific profanities imaginable that they would never use. The foul spirit also tries to make the person degrade themselves, in many cases playing with their own urine or feces, leaving the person mentally disturbed. That is the state that they wish to see their prey in.

The foul spirit often carries with it a rude stench similar to that of garbage, vomit or rotting flesh. Many people have experienced this smell while performing exorcisms during the deliverance of demonic spirits. However, while in ecstatic experiences with God there are accounts of smelling beautiful aromas of honey, incense, frankincense, flowers and sweet smelling fragrances. Song of Solomon 1:3 says, *"Pleasing is the fragrance of your perfumes; your name is like perfume poured out."*

Spirit of Heaviness
Isa 61:3
"To be weighed down, Tired, Under Pressure"

The spirit of heaviness operates in many ways, one being the lack of motivation due to circumstance and situations. This brings about hopelessness to cripple an individual spiritually. This spirit acts as a yoke of oppression and can even feel like a literal weight upon ones shoulders. When the spirit of heaviness is released, the person oftentimes feels lighter physically, emotionally and spiritually. Many who operate under this spirit feel as if they must have an answer for everything and feel like they have to carry everyone else's burdens. Empaths using the discernment of spirits can actually feel this emotional and spiritual baggage carried by individuals around them. When an empath comes in contact with a person under the spirit of heaviness, they could feel this baggage and weight and mistakenly believe that it is their own. This spirit must be dealt with through intercessory prayer and consecration. If not, the spirit will then also linger with the empath who had the supernatural gift to sense its presence. Another way to get free from this spirit's oppression is to offer up the sacrifice of praise unto God. For the scripture says in Isaiah 61:3, *"to give unto them beauty for ashes, the oil of joy for mourning, the garment of praise for the spirit of heaviness; that they might be called trees of righteousness, the planting of the LORD, that he might be glorified."* Praise immediately brings right focus to every circumstance and situation that we are facing and acts as a garment of protection or a hiding place from unclean spirits in the demonic realms.

Part 16
List of Spirits Mentioned and Their Functions

Spirit of Whoredom
Hos 4:12
"Idolatry, Chasing after of other things"

The spirit of whoredom causes one to live and die by the acceptance or rejection of others. It will go from person to person, group to group looking for affirmation that is only found in Father God alone. It is essentially the spirit of prostitution that causes the person to sell themselves short for momentary acceptance. Contextually this term is used when Israel turned her back on Yahweh and went after foreign gods. Most of the time, the person inwardly knows that what they are doing is wrong and they continue to do it to lash out or prove a point to someone. The individual ends up with more baggage than they expected, because they have entered into contracts with beings that have their own interest in mind.

Haughty Spirit
Pro 16:18
"Prideful arrogance"

The haughty spirit is an unteachable spirit. It influences a person to always have to be right, even when proven wrong. Cognitive dissonance is when a person refuses to change their mind or belief, even when shown proof of its falsehood. Operating under cognitive dissonance, the person under the influence of the haughty spirit will cling to a belief tooth and nail, never admitting error in fear of losing validity. This spirit disables a person or teacher from walking in true humility by lording prideful arrogance through doctrine and dogma. It is a controlling spirit of pride, which cometh before a fall.

Spirit of Antichrist
1Jn 4:3
"an *opponent of the Messiah*"

Many people confuse the spirit of antichrist with the antichrist of Revelation. These are two different representations of the same spirit. 1 John 4:3 tells us, "but every spirit that does not acknowledge Jesus is not from God. This is the spirit of the antichrist, which you have heard is coming and even now is already in the world." You will find this spirit abiding within well-meaning people who seem to be some of the nicest people imaginable. Things change when the name of Jesus is mentioned and their countenance begins to change simply over the mention of that name.

Spirit of Divination or Python
Acts 16:16
"a *Python*, (by analogy with the supposed *diviner* there) inspiration (*soothsaying*)"

It can be a little tricky to understand the spirit of Python due to the translation of the Bible. The English the word used is "divination". Divination by itself is not something bad or something to be afraid of. This is not a correct translation because the passage is talking about a woman who is channeling the spirit of Python. The Greek word used here is Python referring to the Pythian serpent that was said to have guarded the oracle at Delphi and that was slain by Apollo. The prophets and disciples all participated in forms of divination and ritual in order to communicate with God. It is all about the intention and manner of which one uses this tool. In the case of the spirit of Python, the texts show us how people are able to channel foreign spirits in order to gain information about people and circumstances. In the end there is usually a high price to pay for this information.

Unclean Spirit
Mat 12:43 & Luk 4:33
"Impure, morally (*lewd*) or specifically (*Devil*)): - foul, unclean."
(See Foul Spirit Mentioned Above)

Spirit of Slumber
Rom 11:8
(Referring To Isa 29:10)
"Perhaps by some confusion"

The spirit of slumber, or spirit of "Deep Sleep" as mentioned in Isaiah 29:10, was sent directly from Yahweh to close the eyes of the prophets and seers. The spirit of slumber was used by God upon the ones who were well learned and well-studied in the wisdom of books and universities. This spirit prevented them from understanding the mysteries of God, because it is not something to be learned from a book. On the contrary, the mysteries of God are to be experienced through the living word of God. The Bible says that God has made it impossible for them that are learned to understand the wisdom of the scriptures. The scripture states that, "Instead, *God chose things the world considers foolish in order to shame those who think they are wise. And he chose things that are powerless to shame those who are powerful"* 1 Corinthians 1:27. We also see this when Jesus chose his disciples from a group of men who were unlearned and rough around the edges. God does this so that we cannot boast in our own understanding and studies. He bids all men to come unto Him and learn and He alone will reveal unto them the things that cannot be fathomed by mortal men, the secrets of Heaven. *"The person without the Spirit does not accept the things that come from the Spirit of God but considers them foolishness, and cannot understand them because they are discerned only through the Spirit."* 1 Corinthians 2:14

Spirit of Error
1Jn 4:6
"Straying from orthodoxy or piety: - deceit, to deceive, delusion"

The spirit of error refers to someone who is being led away into strange doctrine contrary to what has already been established by the apostles. In many cases, this is speaking about straying away from what Paul calls the simplicity of the gospel. Many people who are called into the deep waters of the mysteries of God soon find themselves like Peter. Once they step foot off of the boat, they find themselves sinking in unbelief and trying to rationalize their faith and doubts. This is not a bad thing, it is a part of the process. The way to make sure that you don't sink is to simply do what Peter did while sinking in the ocean of despair. Keep your eyes on Jesus. Do not forsake your first love. Let everything that you do and everything that you share be fueled by the fire of that first love of Christ Jesus. This is what it means to guard your heart. This is also what Paul is referring to in the book of Galatians when he says, "*O foolish Galatians, who hath bewitched you not to obey the truth."* The word bewitched used here is means "to *fascinate* (by false representations)". Many well-meaning people have itching ears and have been led off of the boat only to drown in the sea of forgetfulness.

Part 16
List of Spirits Mentioned and Their Functions

Spirit of Jezebel
Rev 2:20
"to teach and to seduce my servants to commit fornication"

The spirit of Jezebel gets its name from Jezebel, the wife of Ahab, whose main goal was to kill the prophets of God. We learn the way that this spirit operates in the story of Jezebel in the book of 1 Kings. It is by lying, gossip and deception that we see this spirit operating in many churches today. In Revelation 2 we see that this was God's major concern against the Church of Ephesus. They allowed the spirit of Jezebel to roam freely throughout their members. She is a master manipulator and will stop at nothing to silence the prophets of God, both then and now. Jezebel goes after those with a God given voice and brings along with her jealousy and envy. Jealous of the anointing, favor and platform that those around her have, she feels as if she deserves the notoriety and spotlight that is given only by God himself. One of the main ways that Jezebel tries to silence the prophets of God is by means of intimidation. If the person operating under the spirit of Jezebel does not repent, this person must be put out of fellowship in order to keep the fellowship of the saints safe.

Familiar Spirit
1Sa 28:6
"A spirit that has been with ones family in previous generations i.e. Generational Curse (ventriloquist, as from a jar): - bottle,"

The familiar spirit is a spirit who tries to entice men with secrets. Bringing with it the spirit of err, the familiar spirit will entice a person to consult with demonic and unclean spirits through divination and soothsaying in order to get privy information that should come straight from the Father. The spirit knows that men and women thirst for knowledge and the spirit beckons to share it with others for a small fee, yet the price is never worth of consequence of the knowledge. Many new agers practice forms of channeling in which they open themselves up to familiar spirits and allow an entity to speak through them. In Wicca, this spirit is embodied within a spirit animal, which is why black cats are usually kept by practicing witches. Being with a family lineage for generations, this spirit also works to bring the sins of the fathers back unto the children forming generational curses.

Spirit of Infirmity
Luke 13:11

"*feebleness* (of body or mind); by implication *malady*; moral *frailty:* - disease, infirmity, sickness, weakness"

The spirit of infirmity is a spirit of sickness and disease. Jesus knew this and thus knew that mental disorders and ailments usually stemmed from forms of demonic influence. This is why Jesus walked in authority, cleansing people vexed with spirits of infirmities. When a person is vexed with unclean spirits, it can lead to them having hypochondria. This is where the spirits will tell the person that they have many infirmities that they do not really have. This leads to worry and anxiety and will cause health and mental breakdowns.

REFERENCES AND CITATIONS

Vision of Washington - National Tribune, 1880

The Book of Enoch (1906)

Helena Blavatsky (1877). 'Isis Unveiled:

Patrick Cooke – BibleUFO.com

"Contra Vermes," Cod. Vidob. theol. 259

The Recognitions of Clement Chapter XVIII - 4th Century

Testament of Solomon 1st Century CE

Toothy Tumor Found in 1,600-Year-Old Roman Corpse Livescience 2013 - https://www.livescience.com/26446-toothy-tumor-ancient-roman-corpse.html

References and Citations

NOTES AND JOURNALING

Use this section to write your thoughts, feelings, inspirations and insights. Happy Journaling!

Notes and Journaling

Notes and Journaling

Notes and Journaling

Notes and Journaling

Notes and Journaling

Notes and Journaling

Notes and Journaling

Notes and Journaling

Notes and Journaling

Notes and Journaling

ABOUT THE AUTHOR

TruthSeekah is a Christian mystic, author, visionary artist and seer with a vision to release the Spirit of Awakening. Also a songwriter, TruthSeekah has released over 200 songs, each one relating to the subject of spirituality and Christ. His journey has brought him through research and experience with the occult, paranormal, Christianity and the spirit realm. This has led him into many mystical encounters with God, angels, spirits, and many other supernatural beings. As the host of the TruthSeekah Podcast, he has interviewed hundreds of experts and leaders in their fields of supernatural, religious, philosophical, and paranormal studies. TruthSeekah has made it his life's work to understand the spiritual realms and relate it back to people in a practical way. His desire is to help people embrace the reality of the spiritual world so they can walk in supernatural freedom in their lives.

www.TruthSeekah.com

Instagram, Facebook, Twitter | @TruthSeekah

About The Author